Letts

KS3

SUCCESS

SCIENCE

Author

Brian Arnold, Hannah Kingston & Emma Poole

CONTENTS

BIOLOGY

CHEMISTRY

PHYSICS

LIFE PROCESSES AND CELLS

Cells are the building blocks of life. All living things are made up of cells. A living thing is called an organism. Plants and animals are organisms.

IS IT ALIVE?

To be alive you must have the following characteristics:
Movement (plant leaves move towards the Sun).
Respiration (releasing energy from food).
Sensitivity (responding to changes in the environment).
Growth (to adult size).
Reproduction (producing offspring).
Excretion (getting rid of waste products, such as carbon dioxide).
Nutrition (eating).

- Remember these using MRS GREN; or you could make up your own way of remembering.

Examiner's Top Tip
Make sure you know the similarities, and in particular the differences, between an animal and a plant cell.

ANIMAL AND PLANT CELLS

- The cells that make up plants and animals can be seen using a microscope and staining them so they show up more clearly.
- You need to know the differences between them

They both have:
Nucleus
Cytoplasm
Cell membrane

Only plant cells have:
Cell wall
Vacuole
Chloroplasts

animal cell
cytoplasm
nucleus
mitochondria
cell membrane

chloroplast
cytoplasm
nucleus
cell wall
plant cell
cell membrane
vacuole

Nucleus – controls the cell. It controls everything the cell does. The nucleus also contains <u>all the information</u> needed to produce a new living organism.
Cytoplasm – where the <u>chemical reactions</u> take place.
Cell membrane – holds the cell together and controls what passes <u>in</u> and <u>out</u> of the cell.
Cell wall – made of <u>cellulose</u>, which gives a plant cell <u>strength and support</u>.
Vacuole – contains a weak solution of salts and sugar called <u>cell sap</u>.
Chloroplasts – contain a green substance called <u>chlorophyll</u>. This absorbs the Sun's energy so that the plant can <u>make its own food in photosynthesis</u>.

CELLS, TISSUES, ORGANS, ORGAN SYSTEMS

- A group of similar cells working together form a <u>tissue</u>.
- An <u>organ</u> is made up of different tissues working together.
- Organs working together make <u>organ systems</u>.
- Plant cells group together to form tissues and organs until all the cells make up an organism.

SPECIAL CELLS

Some cells can change their shape in order to carry out a particular job. It's a bit like a factory where each person has their own job. It's more efficient this way. One cell can't do everything.

SPECIALISED ANIMAL CELLS

nucleus

cell membrane

- A <u>sperm</u> <u>cell</u> has a <u>tail</u> which enables it to swim towards the egg.

tail

- <u>Red</u> <u>blood</u> <u>cells</u> carry oxygen around the body
- They have <u>no</u> <u>nucleus</u>.

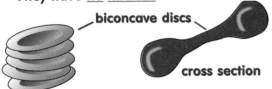

biconcave discs

cross section

- <u>Nerve</u> <u>cells</u> are shaped like wires to conduct messages around the body.

- <u>Egg</u> <u>cells</u> or <u>ova</u> are much larger than sperm. The nucleus contains chromosomes from the mother. In the cytoplasm is yolk, which provides a food store for the developing organism if fertilised

- <u>Ciliated</u> <u>cells</u> line all air passages into your lungs. They produce mucus, which trap dust and bacteria. Tiny hairs called <u>cilia</u> waft the mucus up to the throat to be swallowed.

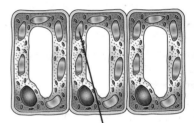

cilia sweep mucus along

a cilated cell

nucleus

SPECIALISED PLANT CELLS

- Root hair cells are <u>long and thin</u>, to absorb water and minerals from the soil.
- They increase the surface area of the roots.

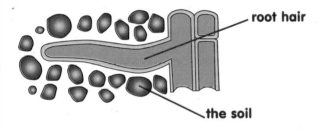

root hair

the soil

- Palisade cells have <u>lots of chloroplasts</u>. They are near the surface of the leaf so they can absorb sunlight for photosynthesis.

lots of chloroplasts

Examiner's Top Tip
Learn the examples of specialised plant and animal cells. Note that they all have a nucleus, cell membrane and a cytoplasm.

QUICK TEST

1. Name three differences between a plant and an animal cell.
2. What does the cell membrane do?
3. What does the cell wall do?
4. What is a specialised cell?
5. A group of similar cells carrying out the same job are called a _____?

5. Tissue.
4. A cell that has changed its shape to do a particular job.
3. Gives a plant cell extra strength and support.
2. It controls what passes in and out of the cell.
1. Plant cell has chloroplasts, cell wall and a vacuole.

PLANT AND HUMAN ORGAN SYSTEMS

PLANT ORGANS

- The plants basic structure is divided up into five parts.
- The parts of a plant have adapted to do a particular job or function.
- The plant carries out all the seven life processes, although they are not quite so obvious.
- Every cell in the plant will carry out respiration.

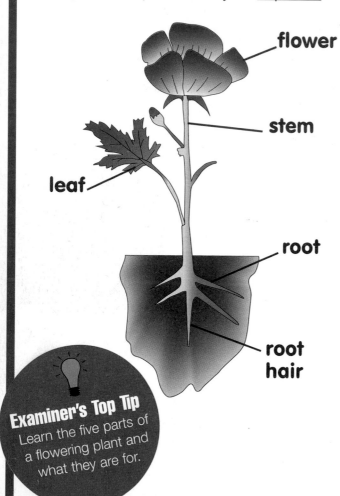

flower

stem

leaf

root

root hair

Examiner's Top Tip
Learn the five parts of a flowering plant and what they are for.

1. THE FLOWER

This contains the male and female sex organs. These make seeds.
The flower is usually brightly coloured to attract insects for pollination.

2. THE STEM

This holds the plant upright.
It contains hollow tubes called xylem and phloem.
Xylem tubes carry water and dissolved minerals from the roots to the leaves.
Phloem carries glucose made by the leaf in photosynthesis up and down the plant.

3. THE ROOT

The root's main job is anchoring the plant in the soil.
They also take up water and minerals from the soil.

4. THE ROOT HAIRS

The actual place where water and minerals are absorbed from the soil.
Root hairs increase the surface area of the roots for more efficient absorption..

5. THE LEAF

- The leaf is the organ of photosynthesis. It makes all the food for the plant.
- The top layer of the leaf contains the palisade cells. This is where most photosynthesis takes place.

- The palisade cells contain lots of chloroplasts. The chloroplasts contain a pigment called chlorophyll. Chlorophyll absorbs sunlight for photosynthesis.
- On the lower surface of the leaf are tiny holes called stomata.

- The stomata open and close to let carbon dioxide in and water vapour and oxygen out.
- The plant is also sensitive to its surroundings, the whole plant will move towards the light.
- If you plant a seed upside down it senses which way to send its shoot and which way to send its root.

HUMAN ORGAN SYSTEMS

- The <u>seven</u> <u>life</u> <u>processes</u> are carried out by different systems in the human body
- There are <u>nine</u> <u>organ</u> <u>systems</u> in the body.
- The following are covered in detail on other pages in this book.

1) The skeletal system
2) The muscle system
3) The respiratory system
4) The digestive system
5) The circulatory system
6) The reproductive system

The three remaining systems are:

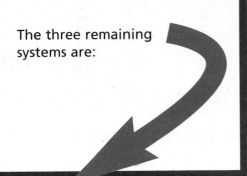

NERVOUS SYSTEM

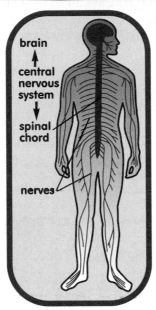

brain

central nervous system

spinal chord

nerves

- We have <u>five</u> <u>sense</u> <u>organs</u> that respond to the environment around us.
- They are the <u>nose</u> (smell), <u>eyes</u> (sight), <u>ear</u> (sound), <u>tongue</u> (taste) and <u>skin</u> (touch).
- All the sense organs contain nerves that detect changes in our surroundings
- The nerves send messages to the brain and spinal cord, which make up the central nervous system
- The brain responds by sending a message back to instruct our muscles what to do.

THE EXCRETORY SYSTEM

- The main organs of excretion are your kidneys.
- Cells produce waste products which go into the blood, some of which are poisonous.
- The kidneys filter and 'clean' the blood by removing these waste products.
- The poisonous waste is turned into <u>urine</u> and stored in the bladder until ready to be released.
- The kidneys control the amount of water going to the bladder so that if you drink too much you produce more urine.

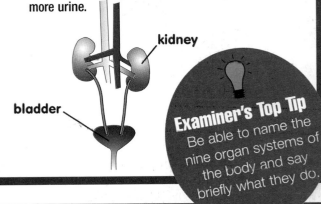

kidney

bladder

Examiner's Top Tip
Be able to name the nine organ systems of the body and say briefly what they do.

ENDOCRINE SYSTEM

- The endocrine system produces <u>hormones</u> in parts of the body called <u>glands</u>.
- The glands release the hormones into the <u>bloodstream</u> where they are carried to where their action is needed.
- Hormones travel a lot slower than nerve messages but their effects are usually longer lasting.
- Hormones control things like <u>menstruation</u> in women as well as the changes that occur to our bodies during puberty.

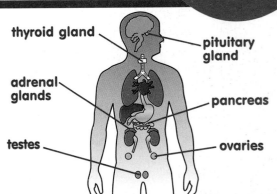

thyroid gland

pituitary gland

adrenal glands

pancreas

testes

ovaries

QUICK TEST

1. What is the job of the leaf?
2. Name the part of the plant that keeps it upright.
3. What is the root's main job?
4. What do the palisade cells contain a lot of?
5. What are the tubes called that transport water and minerals to the leaf?

5. Xylem
4. Chloroplasts/chlorophyll
3. To anchor the plant.
2. Stem
1. Photosynthesis

NUTRITION AND FOOD TESTS

CARBOHYDRATES

- Carbohydrates consist of starch and different types of sugar e.g. glucose (the sugar our bodies use for respiration)
- We need carbohydrates to <u>give us energy</u>.
- Starch is actually made up of smaller glucose molecules joined together. These are foods that contain a lot of carbohydrate:

CHEMICAL TEST FOR STARCH
- Add two drops of yellow/brown <u>iodine solution</u> to food solution.
- Solution will turn blue/black if starch is present.

CHEMICAL TEST FOR GLUCOSE
- Add a few drops of <u>Benedict's solution</u> to food solution.
- Heat in a water bath until it boils.
- If glucose is present, an orange/red precipitate will form.

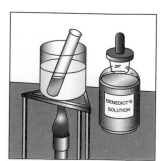

FATS

- Fats are made from fatty acids and glycerol.
- We need fats for a <u>store of energy</u>, to make <u>cell membranes</u> and for <u>warmth</u> (insulation).

These are foods containing a lot of fat:

CHEMICAL TEST FOR FAT
- Add 2 cm³ of <u>ethanol</u> to the food solution in a test tube and shake.
- Add 2 cm³ of <u>water</u> to the test-tube and shake again.
- Fat is present if the solution turns <u>cloudy white</u>.

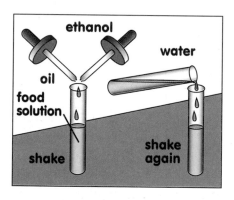

Examiner's Top Tip
Learn the food tests for starch, glucose, protein and fats.

WATER

Water makes up approximately 65% of your body weight.

Water is important because:
- Our blood plasma is mainly water.
- Water is in sweat that cools us down.
- Chemical reactions in our cells take place in water.
- Waste products are removed from our bodies in water.
- Food and drink contain water.

Examiner's Top Tip
Don't forget to learn examples of food belonging to each food group.

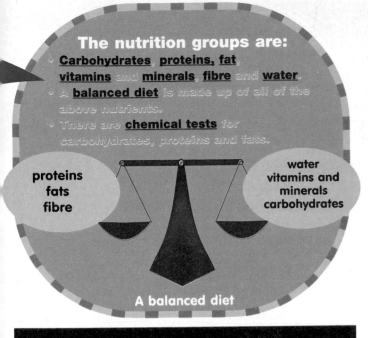

The nutrition groups are:
- Carbohydrates, proteins, fat, vitamins and minerals fibre and water.
- A balanced diet is made up of all of the above nutrients.
- There are chemical tests for carbohydrates, proteins and fats.

proteins fats fibre

water vitamins and minerals carbohydrates

A balanced diet

PROTEIN

- Your body cells are mostly made of protein.
- Proteins are made up of lots of amino acids.
- We need protein to repair and replace damaged cells or to make new cells during growth.

These foods contain a lot of protein:

CHEMICAL TEST FOR PROTEIN, (THE BIURET TEST)

- Add some weak copper sulphate to the food solution.
- Carefully add drops of sodium hydroxide to the solution.
- If protein is present, the solution turns purple, gradually.

VITAMINS AND MINERALS

We only need these in small amounts, but they are essential for good health. Vitamins and minerals are found in fruit, vegetables and cereals. Deficiency diseases are caused by a lack of vitamins and minerals.
Vitamin C keeps the skin strong and supple; without it the skin cracks and the gums bleed (called scurvy).
Vitamin D helps the bones harden in children; without it the bones stay soft (a disease called rickets).
We need the mineral iron for making haemoglobin and the mineral calcium for healthy bones and teeth.

FIBRE

- Fibre, or roughage, comes from plants.
- Fibre is not actually digested; it just keeps food moving smoothly through your system.
- Fibre provides something for your gut muscles to push against. It is a bit like squeezing toothpaste through a tube.
- It prevents constipation.

These are foods containing a lot of fibre:

QUICK TEST

1. What do we use carbohydrates for?
2. What is the chemical test for starch?
3. What is the chemical test for glucose?
4. What do our bodies need fat for?
5. Why is protein important to our cells?
6. What is the chemical test for protein?
7. Why is fibre important?

7. It helps food move through your system and prevents constipation
6. Biuret test; if solution turns purple, protein is present
5. Repair and replace cells, and make new cells for growth
4. Store energy, make cell membranes and insulation
3. Benedict's solution and heat; an orange precipitate means glucose is present
2. Iodine; a blue/black colour means starch is present
1. Energy

THE DIGESTIVE SYSTEM

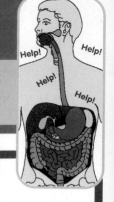

- The digestive system is really one long tube called the gut. If it were unravelled it would be about nine metres long!
- Digestion <u>begins</u> with the <u>teeth</u> and ends at the <u>anus</u>.
- It normally takes food 24–48 hours to pass through your digestive system.

HELP WITH DIGESTION

- Ultimately we need nutrients from our food to keep our bodies healthy.
- Remember: Digestion breaks down large food molecules into small molecules so that they can pass into our bloodstream.
- As food passes through the digestive system it needs help to break it down.

TEETH BEGIN DIGESTION

There are four kinds of teeth, each have a role in <u>breaking up</u> <u>your food</u>:

molars
also chew up your food

premolars
grind and chew your food

incisors
bite your food

canines
tear your food

ENZYMES SPEED THINGS UP

Examiner's Top Tip
Each part of the digestive system has a particular job. Learn the functions of each of the parts and where the enzymes and other helpful secretions are produced.

- Starch, protein and fats are <u>large, insoluble food</u> molecules.
- Even after the teeth have done their bit and the stomach has churned the food up, it is still too big and insoluble to pass into the bloodstream.
- If you look at the diagram of the digestive system on page 11 you will see where these chemicals called <u>enzymes</u> are made.
- Enzymes are specific. There are <u>three main enzymes</u> in your system.

a protein molecule is made up of many different amino acids

protease breaks down protein molecules

amino acids

a starch molecule is made up of many glucose molecules

carbohydrase breaks down carbohydrate molecules

glucose

a fat molecule is made up of fatty acid and glycerol molecules

fatty acid   glycerol

lipase breaks down fat molecules

fatty acids

glycerol

- Food is now small enough to be absorbed through the small intestine wall and into the bloodstream to be carried to the cells.

ABSORPTION

- *The small intestine is where the digested food is absorbed into the blood.*
- *The small intestine is well designed for absorption*

- *It has a <u>thin lining, a good blood supply and a very large surface area</u>.*
- *The large surface area is provided by the villi (single = villus) that extends from the inside of the small intestine wall.*

a villus is only one cell thick

it contains a network of capillaries

blood arriving at the villus to pick up food molecules

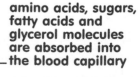

amino acids, sugars, fatty acids and glycerol molecules are absorbed into the blood capillary

blood leaving the villus, taking the food molecules to the rest of the body

DIGESTION

- Digestion is the breaking down of <u>large</u>, <u>insoluble</u> molecules into <u>small</u>, <u>soluble</u> molecules so that they can be absorbed into the bloodstream.
- The large, insoluble molecules are starch, protein and fat.
- This action is speeded up (catalysed) by <u>enzymes</u>.
- Enzymes in the small intestine are found throughout the digestive system.

Examiner's Top Tip
Make sure you can list the organs through which food passes through on a complete journey through the digestive system.

Liver produces bile, a green solution that has two functions: – It <u>neutralises</u> <u>stomach acid</u> so that the enzymes in the small intestine can work properly. (Only pepsin likes acid conditions) – It acts on fats, breaking them up into small droplets. This is called <u>emulsification</u>. Emulsifying fats makes it easier for lipase enzymes to work as they have a larger surface area to work on

6. Large intestine receives any food that has not been absorbed into the blood. Excess water and salts are removed from the food. The remaining solid food is turned into <u>faeces</u>

Rectum where the faeces are stored before they leave the body via the <u>anus</u>

Note: Food does not pass through the <u>pancreas</u>, <u>liver</u> and <u>gall bladder</u>. They are organs that secrete enzymes and bile to help digestion

1. Mouth contains teeth that begin digestion by breaking up food

2. Salivary glands secrete amylase which is a <u>carbohydrase</u> <u>enzyme</u> – Mucus lubricates the food as it passes down the oesophagus

3. Oesophagus sometimes called the gullet

4. Stomach has muscular walls which churn up the food and mix it with the <u>gastric juices</u> that the stomach produces – The gastric juices contain protease enzymes and hydrochloric acid – The hydrochloric acid provides the acidic conditions for a protease enzyme called pepsin to work

Pancreas produces <u>carbohydrase</u>, <u>protease</u> and <u>lipase</u> <u>enzymes</u>

5. Small intestine also produces <u>all</u> <u>three</u> types of enzymes – This is where <u>digestion</u> is <u>completed</u> and dissolved food is <u>absorbed</u> into the bloodstream – The inner surface is covered in tiny finger like projections called <u>villi</u>

QUICK TEST

1. Name the four types of teeth.
2. What does starch get digested into?
3. What does protein get digested into?
4. What do fats get broken down into?
5. Where in the digestive system does the food get absorbed into the blood stream?

1. Incisors, canines, premolars and molars.
2. Glucose
3. Amino acids
4. Fatty acids and glycerol.
5. Small intestine.

VEINS

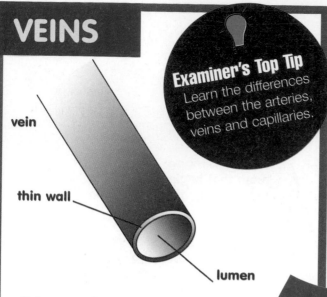

vein

thin wall

lumen

- *Veins carry <u>deoxygenated</u> blood.*
- *The <u>pulmonary</u> <u>vein</u> is the only vein to <u>carry oxygenated</u> <u>blood</u>. This is because it has just been to the lungs. Find it on the diagram.*
- *They carry the blood <u>back</u> <u>to</u> <u>the</u> <u>heart</u> from the body at low pressure.*
- *They have <u>valves</u> to prevent the blood flowing backwards.*

longitudinal section of vein

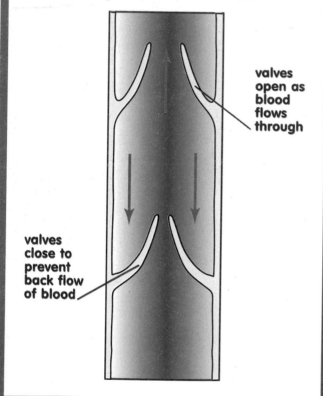

valves open as blood flows through

valves close to prevent back flow of blood

THE HEART

- The heart is a double pump.
- It has four chambers, the top two are the left and right atriums and the bottom two are the left and right ventricles.
- The right side pumps blood to the lungs to be <u>oxygenated</u>.
- The left side pumps blood around the body and it becomes <u>deoxygenated</u> as it drops off oxygen to the cells

VEINS = IN

CAPILLARIES

- **Capillaries are only <u>one cell thick</u> and have very thin walls, to allow oxygen and nutrients to diffuse out of them.**
- **They are the site of exchange between the blood and the cells of the body.**

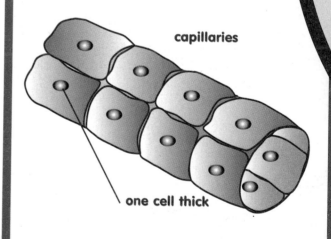

capillaries

one cell thick

CORONARY HEART DISEASE

- The coronary arteries supply the heart with oxygen and nutrients.
- Excess cholesterol, alcohol, stress and smoking all contribute to blocking these arteries.
- Excess cholesterol can 'fur' up the arteries and block blood flow. This can result in a heart attack.

ARTERIES

- Arteries carry <u>oxygenated</u> blood.
- The <u>pulmonary artery</u> is the only artery to carry <u>deoxygenated blood</u>. This is because it is going to the lungs to pick up oxygen. Find it on the diagram.
- They carry blood <u>away</u> from the heart towards the body at <u>high pressure</u>.
- They have very <u>thick</u>, <u>elastic walls</u> to withstand the high pressure.
- The high pressure in the arteries causes a <u>pulse</u> that can be felt especially in the wrist and neck.
- Arteries narrow down into capillaries.

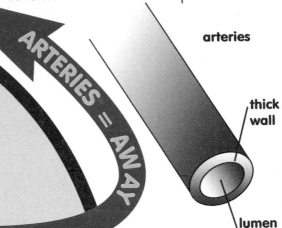

arteries

thick wall

lumen

ARTERIES = AWAY

GETTING TO THE HEART OF THE MATTER

- The heart has its own blood supply called coronary arteries.

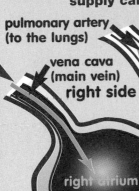

pulmonary artery (to the lungs)

vena cava (main vein) **right side**

left side

aorta (main artery – to the body)

pulmonary vein (from the lungs)

left atrium

right atrium

semilunar valves

right ventricle

left ventricle (has thicker walls than the right ventricle)

FOUR KEY POINTS TO REMEMBER...

1. <u>Arteries</u> carry blood <u>away</u> from the heart.
2. <u>Veins</u> carry blood back <u>into</u> the heart.
3. The <u>left side</u> of the heart receives <u>oxygenated</u> blood.
4. The <u>right side</u> of the heart receives <u>deoxygenated</u> blood.

QUICK TEST

1. Which blood vessels carry blood away from the heart?
2. Which blood vessels carry blood back to the heart?
3. Name two blood vessels that enter the heart.
4. Name two blood vessels that leave the heart
5. What are valves for?

5. To prevent back flow of blood in the heart and the veins.
4. Pulmonary artery and aorta
3. Pulmonary vein and vena cava
2. Veins
1. Arteries

WHITE BLOOD CELLS

- Their main function is <u>defence</u> <u>against</u> <u>disease</u>.
- They are larger than red blood cells and do have a nucleus.

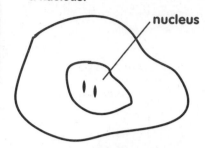

nucleus

Examiner's Top Tip
Learn the functions of the four parts of the blood.

blood is made up of
white cells
red cells   platelets

floating in a watery
liquid called plasma

RED BLOOD CELLS

- *Their function is to <u>carry</u> <u>oxygen</u> to all the cells of the body.*
- *They contain a substance called <u>haemoglobin</u>.*
- *They have <u>no</u> <u>nucleus</u> (more room for oxygen).*

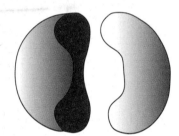

this diagram shows a red blood cell that has been sectioned to show its characteristic shape

PLATELETS

- Platelets are fragments of cells.
- Their function is to <u>clot</u> <u>the</u> <u>blood</u> so you do not bleed to death if you cut yourself.

PLASMA

- Plasma is a yellow fluid.
- It consists of mainly water, but has many substances dissolved in it. These include <u>soluble food</u>, <u>salts</u>, <u>carbon dioxide</u>, <u>urea</u>, <u>hormones</u>, <u>antibodies</u> and <u>plasma proteins</u>.
- Its function is to transport these substances around the body.

EXCHANGE OF SUBSTANCES

- The blood flows round the circulatory system in the blood vessels.
- 1. The arteries narrow down into capillaries and bring oxygen and dissolved food to all the cells of the body.
- 2. The cells can only exchange substances in the capillary networks of the body.
- 3. The capillaries then join up to form veins that take the blood back to the heart.
- This is what happens at the cells, oxygen and food diffuse into the cells from the capillaries and waste and carbon dioxide diffuse out of the cells into the capillaries.

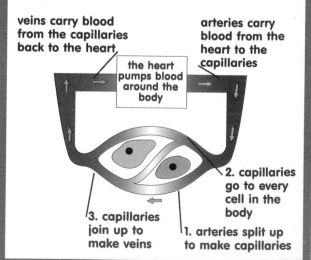

veins carry blood from the capillaries back to the heart

arteries carry blood from the heart to the capillaries

the heart pumps blood around the body

2. capillaries go to every cell in the body

3. capillaries join up to make veins

1. arteries split up to make capillaries

BLOOD AND CIRCULATORY SYSTEM

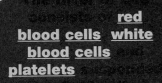

The blood of life consists of <u>red blood cells</u>, <u>white blood cells</u> and <u>platelets</u> suspended in a fluid called <u>plasma</u>

- The <u>circulatory system</u> transports substances around the body to where they are needed and removes waste products.
- The heart is a <u>pump</u> that pushes the blood around the circulatory system.

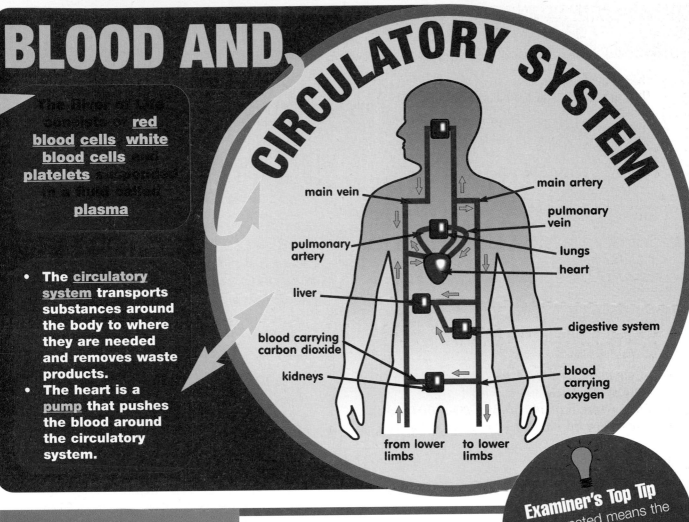

CIRCULATORY SYSTEM

- main vein
- main artery
- pulmonary vein
- pulmonary artery
- lungs
- heart
- liver
- digestive system
- blood carrying carbon dioxide
- kidneys
- blood carrying oxygen
- from lower limbs
- to lower limbs

Examiner's Top Tip
Oxygenated means the blood has oxygen, deoxygenated means the blood has given up its oxygen to the cells.

CIRCULATION

- The blood follows a specific route through the heart and around the body
- This is to ensure all parts of the body get the substances they need and get waste substances removed.
- We have a <u>double circulation system</u>. The blood passes through the heart twice on one circuit of the body.
- The heart has two sides that act as two separate pumps.
- The <u>left side</u> of the heart has much <u>thicker, walled ventricles</u> as this side has to pump blood at high pressure all around the body.
- Follow the passage of blood as it leaves the heart on the left side.
  1. The main artery of the heart, the aorta takes oxygenated blood to the capillaries in the body.
  2. The deoxygenated blood delivers oxygen and food to the body cells and collects waste and carbon dioxide
  3. The deoxygenated blood travels back to the right side of the heart in the main vein, the vena cava.
  4. The blood then leaves the heart in the pulmonary artery to collect oxygen from the lungs.
  5. The pulmonary vein brings oxygenated blood back to the heart and the cycle begins again.

QUICK TEST

1. What four main things does blood contain?
2. Which type of cell has no nucleus?
3. Which side of the heart contains oxygenated blood?
4. Why does the blood go to the lungs?
5. Why is it called a double circulation system?

5. Because blood passes through the heart twice.
4. To collect oxygen/to release CO₂.
3. The left.
2. Red blood cells
1. Plasma, red blood cells, white blood cells and platelets.

SKELETON, MUSCLES AND JOINTS

THE SKELETON

- The skeleton is made of bones that are strong and rigid.
- Bones are shaped like tubes; the hollow part in the middle is filled with bone marrow.
- The skeleton of many animals including humans has three important roles to play:
1. Support – without the skeleton we would fall to the floor.
2. Protection – the skeleton protects our organs. The skull protects the brain and the ribs protect the heart and lungs.
3. Movement – many parts of the skeleton are jointed so that movement can take place. Movements are made by muscles. Muscles are attached to the skeleton by tendons.

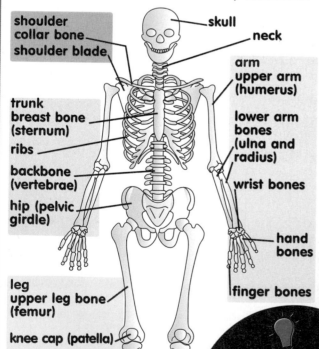

shoulder
collar bone
shoulder blade

skull

neck

arm
upper arm
(humerus)

trunk
breast bone
(sternum)

ribs

lower arm
bones
(ulna and
radius)

backbone
(vertebrae)

wrist bones

hip (pelvic
girdle)

hand
bones

finger bones

leg
upper leg bone
(femur)

knee cap (patella)

lower leg bones
(tibia and fibula)

ankle bones

foot bones

toe bones

Examiner's Top Tip
Don't rush through the labelled diagrams: make sure you understand them and are able to label them yourself if they are in the exam.

JOINTS

Joints occur when two bones meet. They allow movement. The bones are held together by strong fibres called ligaments.
There are several different types of joint:
1. Hinge – e.g. knee joint, elbow joint, wrist joint.
2. Ball and socket – e.g. hip joint, shoulder joint.
3. Partly moveable – e.g. the spine.
4. Fixed – e.g. the skull.
Ball and socket and hinge joints are also known as synovial joints.
The ends of the bone in these joints have a layer of smooth cartilage.
Cartilage acts as a shock absorber that prevents the wearing away of the surfaces. The cartilage is covered by synovial fluid.
Synovial fluid helps reduce friction at the joint.

Examiner's Top Tip
Remember tendons join muscles to bone and ligaments join bone to bone.

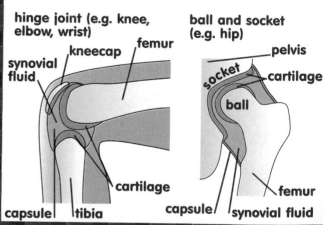

hinge joint (e.g. knee, elbow, wrist)

synovial fluid

kneecap

femur

cartilage

capsule | tibia

ball and socket (e.g. hip)

pelvis

socket

cartilage

ball

femur

capsule | synovial fluid

REFLEX ACTIONS

- Often the messages from the sense organs are sent very quickly to the brain and back again.
- For example, if you touch something hot you automatically, without thinking, move your hand away.
- This is called a reflex action and often protects you from harm.

MUSCLES

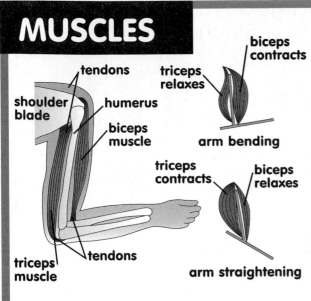

shoulder blade
humerus
tendons
biceps muscle
triceps muscle
tendons

biceps contracts
triceps relaxes
arm bending

triceps contracts
biceps relaxes
arm straightening

- The muscles provide the force needed to move the bones at joints.
- Muscles can only pull; they cannot push.
- When a muscle pulls it gets shorter and fatter: it <u>contracts</u>.
- When a muscle is not contracting it relaxes and returns to its normal size.
- Muscles all over the body work in pairs; while one contracts the other relaxes.
- These are called <u>antagonistic pairs</u> because they work in opposite directions to produce movement.
- Muscles are attached to bones by <u>tendons</u>.
- An example of an antagonistic muscle pair is the <u>triceps</u> and <u>biceps</u> of the arms.

CONTROL OF MOVEMENT

In order for muscles to move parts of your body they have to be told what to do. Your body is controlled by the central nervous system (the brain and spinal cord). The <u>central nervous system</u> is linked to the rest of the body by <u>nerves</u>. Messages travel along these nerves to the central nervous system and back to the muscle to tell it what to do.

We have sense organs that detect changes to our environment and send messages to the brain.

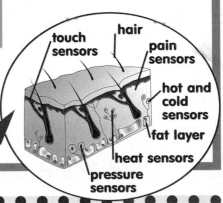

spinal cord and brain
muscle
heat sensors in the skin

Our <u>sense organs</u> are:	They respond to:
• eyes	• light
• nose	• chemicals in the air
• ears	• sound
• tongue	• chemicals in food
• skin	• touch, pressure, heat and pain

- Our skin covers the whole of our body, so it is in contact with the outside environment. It has many <u>sensors</u>.
- The skin also has a fat layer for insulation; in hairy animals the hair also traps air for extra insulation.

touch sensors
hair
pain sensors
hot and cold sensors
fat layer
heat sensors
pressure sensors

17

THE LUNGS AND BREATHING

- The lungs are two big air sacs in your upper body.
- Their job is to supply <u>oxygen to your cells when you breathe in</u> and get rid of the waste product carbon dioxide when you breathe out.
- This is called <u>gas exchange</u>.

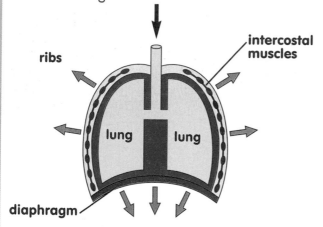

blood capillaries

alveoli

air space

The intercostal muscles in between the ribs assist with breathing movements.

trachea

The heart lies in between the lungs.

The ribs protect the lungs.

The diaphragm is a sheet of muscle that helps breathing.

The trachea branches into two bronchi, each called a bronchus. They divide up, one to each lung.

The bronchi split up into many smaller branches called bronchioles.

The branches end at tiny air sacs called alveoli. The alveoli are where gas exchange takes place.

Examiner's Top Tip
Learn the labelled diagram of the lungs.

BREATHING IN

- Ribs move up and out pulled by the intercostal muscles.
- The diaphragm gets pulled down.
- The volume increases causing air to rush into the lungs.

ribs

intercostal muscles

lung   lung

diaphragm

BREATHING OUT

- The intercostal muscles relax and the ribs move down and in.
- The diaphragm also relaxes and moves up.
- The volume decreases and air is forced out of the lungs.

ribs

intercostal muscles

lung   lung

diaphragm

The movement of air into and out of the lungs is called <u>ventilation</u>.

ALVEOLI AND GAS EXCHANGE

- The alveoli are well designed for their job of gas exchange.
- There are millions of alveoli, so they present a <u>large surface area</u>; they are in <u>very close contact</u> with lots of blood capillaries.
- Their surface lining is moist, so that the gases can dissolve before they diffuse across the <u>thin membrane</u>.
- At the lungs, oxygen diffuses into the blood and carbon dioxide diffuses into the alveoli.
- At the cells, oxygen diffuses into them and carbon dioxide diffuses out into the blood.

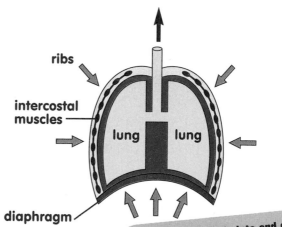

inhaled air

exhaled air

'wall' of alveolus is very thin

thin film of moisture on inside of alveolus

respiring cells using oxygen

respiring cells making carbon dioxide

blood carries oxygen from lungs to cells

blood carries carbon dioxide from cells to lungs

COMPOSITION OF GASES

IN INHALED AIR	IN EXHALED AIR
Oxygen – 21%	Oxygen – 16%
Carbon dioxide – 0.04%	Carbon dioxide – 4%
Nitrogen – 79%	Nitrogen – 79%
Water vapour – a little	Water vapour – a lot

NOTE
- Notice that we breathe out oxygen and carbon dioxide as well as breathing them both in.
- It is important to note that we breathe in <u>more</u> oxygen and breathe out <u>more</u> carbon dioxide.
- There are other differences: the air we breathe out contains more water vapour and it is warmer and cleaner compared to the air we breathe in.

RESPIRATION

- Breathing is necessary for <u>respiration</u>.
- Respiration is <u>not</u> breathing in and out.
- Respiration is a chemical reaction that <u>breaks</u> <u>down</u> <u>glucose</u> <u>from</u> <u>food</u> <u>to</u> <u>release</u> <u>energy</u> <u>using</u> <u>oxygen</u>.
- Every living cell in every living organism uses respiration to make <u>energy</u>, all of the time.
- <u>Carbon</u> <u>dioxide</u> <u>and</u> <u>water</u> <u>are</u> <u>waste</u> <u>products</u> removed from the body in the lungs, skin and kidneys.
- Respiration takes place inside the <u>cytoplasm</u> of cells.

oxygen, food → carbon dioxide, water

- The chemical equation for respiration is:

$$C_6H_{12}O_6 + 6O_2 \rightarrow 6CO_2 + 6H_2O + \underline{energy}$$

And the word equation is:

Glucose + Oxygen → Carbon Dioxide + Water + <u>energy</u>

SMOKING AND LUNG DISEASE

- Tar contained in tobacco smoke can cause cancer of the lung cells. It can also irritate air passages and make them narrower, causing a 'smoker's cough'.
- Bronchitis is aggravated by smoking. Smoke irritates the air passages making them inflamed. The cilia stop beating, so mucus collects in the lungs along with dirt and bacteria.
- Emphysema is when the chemicals in tobacco smoke weaken the alveoli walls. The lung tissue can become damaged and make breathing difficult.

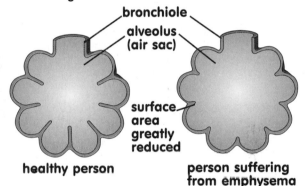

bronchiole
alveolus (air sac)
surface area greatly reduced
healthy person
person suffering from emphysema

USES OF THE ENERGY PRODUCED

- The energy produced during respiration is used for:
1. Making your muscles work.
2. Uptake of minerals in plants.
3. Chemical reactions.
4. Growth and repair of cells.
5. Maintaining body temperature in warm-blooded animals.

Examiner's Top Tip
Learn the word equation for respiration.

QUICK TEST
1. Where does gas exchange take place?
2. Why are the alveoli so good at gas exchange?
3. Give a definition of aerobic respiration.
4. Where does respiration take place?
5. What are the waste products of respiration?

5. Water and carbon dioxide.
4. In the cell cytoplasm.
3. Breaking down glucose with oxygen.
2. They have a large surface area, moist, thin walls and are close to blood capillaries.
1. In the alveoli of the lungs.

ADOLESCENCE AND THE MENSTRUAL CYCLE

- Adolescence is a time in people's lives where the body changes from a child to an adult. Emotions also change
- Puberty is the first stage of adolescence, most changes occur at this time.
- Puberty usually begins at the age of 10–14 in girls and a little older in boys. Not everybody starts puberty at the same time.

PUBERTY

Physical changes that take place during puberty include:

BOYS
- Testes start to produce sperm and a hormone called testosterone.
- Penis grows larger.
- Body hair appears on the face, chest, armpits and around the penis.
- Voice gets deeper.
- Skin produces more oil that blocks pores and causes spots.

GIRLS
- Ovaries start to release eggs and produce a hormone called oestrogen.
- Breasts grow larger.
- Body hair grows under the arms and around the vagina.
- Skin produces more oil that blocks pores and causes spots.
- Menstruation begins.

EMOTIONAL CHANGES
- Boys and girls also go through emotional changes caused by changing levels of hormones.
- Behaviour changes occur such as irritability and mood swings and they develop an interest in the opposite sex.

THE HUMAN REPRODUCTIVE SYSTEM

- During puberty, males produce sperm and females start to release eggs.
- Sperm is made in the testes.
- During sexual intercourse the penis becomes erect and sperms are then ejaculated into the vagina.
- The sperms swim up towards the fallopian tube to meet an egg
- An egg is released once a month by alternate ovaries and moves down the fallopian tube.
- If sexual intercourse takes place then sperm is released into the vagina.
- In the fallopian tube the egg may meet a sperm and get fertilised.
- If the egg is not fertilised then it will pass out of the vagina during menstruation.

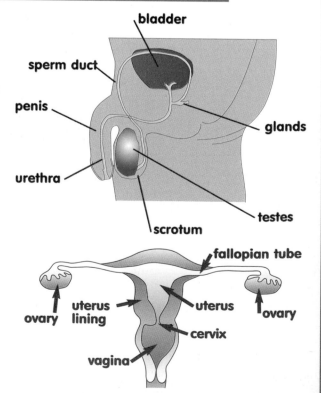

THE MENSTRUAL CYCLE

- *A sequence of events occurs each month in females called the menstrual cycle.*
- *The menstrual cycle lasts approximately <u>28</u> <u>days</u>.*
- *The menstrual cycle involves preparing the uterus to receive a fertilised egg.*
- *If fertilisation doesn't happen then the egg and the lining of the uterus break down and leave the body through the vagina.*
- *This is sometimes called having a <u>period</u> and lasts between <u>four</u> and <u>seven</u> days.*

THE STAGES OF THE MENSTRUAL CYCLE

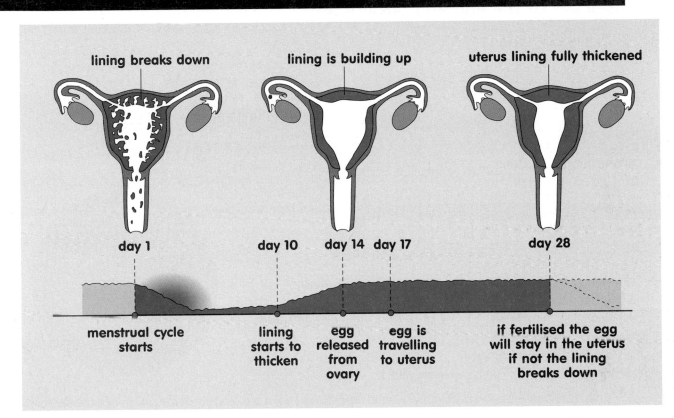

lining breaks down | lining is building up | uterus lining fully thickened

day 1 | day 10 | day 14 | day 17 | day 28

menstrual cycle starts | lining starts to thicken | egg released from ovary | egg is travelling to uterus | if fertilised the egg will stay in the uterus if not the lining breaks down

<u>Day</u> <u>1–5</u>: A menstrual bleed (a period) occurs and the lining of the uterus breaks down.

<u>Day</u> <u>5–14</u>: The uterus lining builds up again and becomes thicker with lots of blood vessels. This is to prepare for implantation (see page 22).

<u>Day</u> <u>14</u>: The ovary releases an egg called ovulation.

<u>Day</u> <u>14–28</u>: The uterus lining is maintained in case a fertilised egg arrives. If no fertilisation occurs then the cycle begins again and a period happens.

Examiner's Top Tip
Learn the diagrams well enough so that you will be able to label them in the exam.

QUICK TEST

1. Where are the sperms made?
2. Where are the eggs made?
3. How often does menstruation take pIace?
4. What is ovulation?
5. How long does a period usually last?
6. What are the two hormones produced during puberty?

6. Testosterone and oestrogen.
5. Four to seven days.
4. The release of an egg on approximately day 14 of the cycle.
3. Every 28 days
2. Ovaries
1. Testes

FERTILISATION

- As part of the female menstrual cycle an egg is released at around the middle of the cycle, called <u>ovulation</u>.
- When a man and a woman have <u>sexual intercourse</u> sperm from the penis of the man passes into the vagina of the woman.
- The sperms swim up to the uterus and into the fallopian tubes to meet an egg.
- Many sperms die along the way. Only one sperm is able to break through the cell membrane of the egg and fertilise it.
- If a sperm meets an egg then fertilisation takes place.
- Fertilisation is the <u>fusing together</u> of the <u>sperm nucleus</u> and the <u>egg nucleus</u>.
- Fertilisation takes place in the <u>fallopian tube</u>.

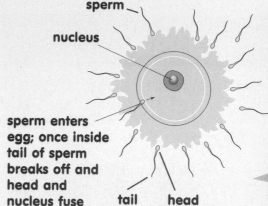

sperm

nucleus

sperm enters egg; once inside tail of sperm breaks off and head and nucleus fuse

tail   head

AFTER FERTILISATION

- The fertilised egg divides into a ball of cells as it passes down the fallopian tube.
- The ball of cells become an <u>embryo</u> and embeds itself into the uterus lining. This is called <u>implantation</u>.
- The embryo develops into a baby
- At about nine weeks the embryo is now called a <u>foetus</u>.

DEVELOPMENT AND PROTECTION

- During the development of the foetus it is provided with food and oxygen by the <u>umbilical cord</u>.
- Waste materials from the foetus pass back along the umbilical cord.
- The blood of the foetus and the mother do not mix but they pass close together to allow exchange of food, oxygen and wastes.
- The <u>placenta</u> is an organ that grows early in the pregnancy. It acts as barrier preventing harmful substances reaching the foetus.
- The foetus is attached to the placenta by the umbilical cord.
- The baby is protected inside the uterus by a sac filled with a watery liquid, called the <u>amniotic fluid</u>.
- The fluid acts as a shock absorber against minor bumps.

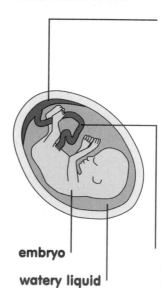

placenta: here the embryo's vessels are close to the mother's and food and oxygen diffuse into the embryo and waste products diffuse out

embryo

watery liquid

umbilical cord: this connects the baby to its mother

BIRTH AND AFTER

- After nine months of pregnancy the baby is ready to be born through the vagina.
- The baby normally turns so that its head is down towards the <u>cervix</u>.
- Muscles in the wall of the uterus begin to contract and the cervix widens
- The baby's head passes through the cervix when it is wide enough into the vagina.
- The fluid sac bursts and the watery liquid runs out.
- More contractions push the baby out of the vagina
- More contractions push the placenta out. This is called the <u>afterbirth</u>.
- The umbilical cord is cut and the baby has to breathe for itself.

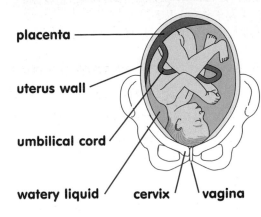

placenta

uterus wall

umbilical cord

watery liquid   cervix   vagina

REPRODUCTION

- Human reproduction involves the joining together of a male sperm and a female egg in a process called <u>fertilisation</u>.
- The fertilised egg implants itself into the uterus lining and begins its development into a baby.
- A human pregnancy lasts approximately nine months or 40 weeks.

TWINS

- <u>Identical</u> twins are formed if the fertilised egg divides into two, and each part develops into a baby.
- <u>Non-identical</u> twins are formed when two eggs are released from the ovary and both are fertilised.

QUICK TEST

1. What is a fertilised egg called?
2. What is implantation?
3. Where does fertilisation take place?
4. What is fertilisation?
5. How is the foetus supplied with oxygen and food while in the uterus?
6. How long does a human pregnancy usually last?

6. Nine months/40 weeks
5. By the umbilical cord
4. The fusing together of the sperm nucleus with the egg nucleus.
3. In the fallopian tube
2. The embryo embedding itself into the uterus lining.
1. An embryo

DRUGS, SOLVENTS, ALCOHOL AND TOBACCO

- Smoking and solvents damage health without a doubt
- Alcohol and drugs are also dangerous if misused.
- To keep healthy you need to eat a balanced diet, take regular exercise and avoid health risks.

DRUGS – WHY ARE THEY DANGEROUS?

- Drugs are powerful chemicals; they alter the way the body works, often without you realising it.
- There are useful drugs such as penicillin and antibiotics, but these can be dangerous if misused.
- <u>Some</u> <u>drugs</u> <u>affect</u> <u>the</u> <u>brain</u> <u>and</u> <u>nervous</u> <u>system</u>, which in turn affect activities such as driving, behaviour and risk of infection.
- Drugs affect people in many different ways; you can never be sure what will happen to you.
- An overdose can easily happen by accident as it is difficult to tell how strong a drug is or how much to take.
- Drugs which affect the brain fall into four main groups:

SEDATIVES
- These drugs <u>slow</u> <u>down</u> <u>the</u> <u>brain</u> and make you feel sleepy. Tranquillisers and sleeping pills are examples.
- They are often given to people suffering from anxiety and stress.
- Barbiturates, which are powerful sedatives, are used as anaesthetics in hospitals.
- These drugs seriously alter reaction times and give you poor judgement of speed and distances.

PAINKILLERS
- These drugs suppress the pain sensors in the brain.
- Aspirin, heroin and morphine are examples.

- Morphine is given to people in cases of extreme pain.
- Heroin can be injected, which can increase the risk of contracting HIV; it is also highly addictive. People who become addicted to heroin often resort to crime to pay for the drug and suffer personality problems.

HALLUCINOGENS
- These drugs make you see or hear things that don't exist. These imaginings are called hallucinations.
- Examples are ecstasy, LSD and cannabis.
- The hallucinations can lead to fatal accidents.
- Ecstasy can give the user feelings of extreme energy. This extra energy can lead to a danger of overheating and dehydration.

STIMULANTS
- These drugs speed up the brain and nervous system and make you more alert and awake.
- Examples include amphetamines, cocaine and the less harmful caffeine in tea and coffee.
- Overuse results in high energy levels, changes in personality and hallucinations.
- Dependence on these drugs is high and withdrawing use causes serious depression.

Examiner's Top Tip
Concentrate on the health problems for the exam, but the social aspects are still important.

ALCOHOL

- *Alcohol is a legal drug and socially acceptable but it can still cause a lot of harm.*
- *Alcohol is a <u>depressant</u> and reduces the activity of the brain and nervous system.*
- *It is absorbed through the gut and taken to the brain in the blood.*
- *Alcohol damages brain cells causing irreversible brain damage.*
- *Alcohol can destroy parts of the liver and cause a disease called <u>cirrhosis</u>.*
- *Increasing amounts of alcohol cause people to lose control and slur their words. In this state accidents are more likely to happen.*
- *Alcohol can become very addictive without the person thinking they have a problem.*

SOLVENTS

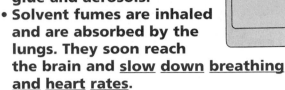

- Solvents include everyday products like glue and aerosols.
- Solvent fumes are inhaled and are absorbed by the lungs. They soon reach the brain and <u>slow</u> <u>down</u> <u>breathing and</u> <u>heart rates</u>.
- Solvents also damage the <u>kidneys and</u> <u>liver</u>.
- Repeated inhalation can cause loss of control and unconsciousness.
- Many first-time inhalers die from heart failure or suffocation if using aerosols.
- Many of the symptoms are likened to being drunk, vomiting may occur and the person may not be in control.

SMOKING

- Tobacco definitely causes health problems.
- It contains many harmful chemicals: <u>nicotine</u> is an addictive substance and a mild stimulant; <u>tar</u> is known to contain carcinogens that <u>contribute</u> to cancer; and <u>carbon</u> <u>monoxide</u> prevents the red blood cells from carrying oxygen.
- Some diseases aggravated by smoking include <u>emphysema</u>, <u>bronchtis</u>, <u>heart</u> <u>and</u> <u>blood</u> <u>vessel</u> <u>problems</u> <u>and</u> <u>lung</u> <u>cancer</u>.
- As well as health problems there is also the high cost of smoking and the negative social problems.

QUICK TEST

1. Which parts of the body are affected by alcohol?
2. What are stimulants?
3. Name three chemicals contained in tobacco.
4. What diseases does smoking aggravate?
5. What is the name of the disease of the liver caused by drinking excess alcohol?

5. Cirrhosis
4. Emphysema, bronchitis, lung cancer and heart disease
3. Tar, nicotine and carbon monoxide
2. Drugs that speed up the nervous syste
1. Brain, liver and nervous system

BACTERIA

- Bacteria are living organisms.
- There are three main shapes of bacteria:

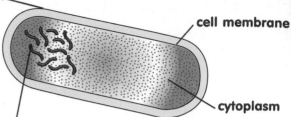

cell wall
cell membrane
cytoplasm

bacterial cells have <u>no</u> <u>nucleus</u> but do have genes in the cytoplasm

rods (bacilli)   spheres (cocci)   spirals (spirilla)

- Bacteria reproduce rapidly.
- Bacteria can produce poisons, called <u>toxins</u>. For example, food poisoning is caused by bacteria releasing toxins.
- Other diseases caused by bacteria include tetanus, whooping cough and tuberculosis.
- Most bacteria are killed by antibiotics.

FUNGI

- *Fungi cause diseases such as athlete's foot and ringworm.*
- *Fungi reproduce by <u>making spores</u> that can be carried from person to person.*
- *Most fungi are useful as decomposers. Yeast is a fungus that is used when making bread, beer and wine.*

VIRUSES

Viruses consist of a <u>protein coat</u> surrounding a few <u>genes</u>.

protein coat

genetic material (not in a nucleus)

- Viruses are much smaller than bacteria.
- Viruses don't feed, move, respire or grow; they just reproduce.
- Viruses can only survive inside the cells of a living organism.
- They <u>reproduce inside the cells</u> and release thousands of new viruses to infect new cells.
- They <u>kill the cell</u> in the process.

virus enters cell   virus reproduces   cell bursts – viruses invade new cells

virus   cell

- Examples of diseases caused by viruses are HIV, flu, chicken pox and measles.

DEFENCE AGAINST DISEASE

- Microbes have to enter our body before they can do any harm.
- The human body has many methods of <u>preventing microbes</u> from entering the body, such as your skin.
- If microbes do get in then the body then your <u>immune system</u> goes into action.

Examiner's Top Tip
Learn how the white blood cells fight infection.

FIGHTING DISEASE

- Microbes are <u>bacteria</u>, <u>viruses</u> and <u>fungi</u>.
- Not all microbes cause disease; some are useful.
- Microbes that get inside you and make you feel ill are called <u>germs</u>.

THE IMMUNE SYSTEM RESPONSE

If the microbes get into the body then your <u>white</u> <u>blood</u> <u>cells</u> travelling around in your blood spring into action.

- White blood cells can make chemicals called <u>antitoxins</u> that destroy the toxins produced by bacteria.
- White blood cells <u>engulf</u> the odd bacteria or viruses before they have a chance to do any harm.
- However, if the microbes are there in large numbers then another type of white blood cell produces <u>antibodies</u> to fight them.

Microbes have <u>foreign</u> <u>antigens</u> on their surface.
<u>Antibodies</u> attach to the microbes antigens clump them together, they can then be engulfed and destroyed.

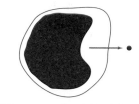

this type of white blood cell sends out antibodies which kill microbes

this type of white blood cell kills microbes by ingesting them

NATURAL IMMUNITY

- Making antibodies takes time which is why you feel ill at first and then get better as the disease is destroyed by the white blood cells and antibodies.

- Once a particular antibody is made it stays in your body. If the same disease enters your body the antibodies are much quicker at destroying it and you feel no symptoms. <u>You</u> <u>are</u> <u>now</u> <u>immune</u> <u>to</u> <u>that</u> <u>disease</u>.

ARTIFICIAL IMMUNITY

- Artificial immunity involves the use of vaccines.
- <u>A</u> <u>vaccine</u> <u>contains</u> <u>dead</u> <u>or</u> <u>harmless</u> <u>microbes</u>.
- These microbes still have antigens on them and your white blood cells respond to them as if they were alive by multiplying and producing antibodies.

- A vaccine is an advanced warning so that if the person is infected by the microbe the white blood cells can <u>respond</u> <u>immediately</u> and kill them.

Examiner's Top Tip
Make sure you know the difference between natural immunity and artificial immunity.

QUICK TEST

1. Name the three main types of microbes.
2. What chemicals do white blood cells produce?
3. What are vaccines?
4. Name two diseases caused by viruses.
5. Name two diseases caused by bacteria.

5. Food poisoning, tuberculosis, whooping cough (any two)
4. HIV, colds, flu, chicken pox, measles (any two)
3. Dead or weak forms of a disease that give you artificial immunity.
2. Antitoxins and antibodies.
1. Bacteria, viruses and fungi.

PHOTOSYNTHESIS

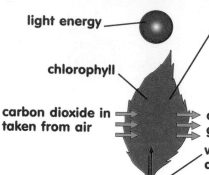

- All living things need food: animals have to find their food and plants make their own.

light energy

glucose made in leaves is taken to all parts of plant

chlorophyll

carbon dioxide in taken from air

oxygen is given out

water and minerals are taken in from soil by plant's roots

- Photosynthesis is a <u>chemical process</u> that plants use to make their food (glucose) using energy from the Sun. It occurs in the leaves.
- Leaves then use this food to generate other useful substances and to obtain energy through respiration.
- Photosynthesis occurs in the light and respiration occurs all of the time.

Examiner's Top Tip
It is very important to learn the word equation for photosynthesis.

The <u>word</u> <u>equation</u> of <u>photosynthesis</u>:

light
carbon dioxide + water $\Rightarrow$ glucose + oxygen
chlorophyll

The balanced symbol equation is:

$6CO_2 + 6H_2O \Rightarrow C_6H_{12}O_6 + 6O_2$

THE LEAF – THE ORGAN OF PHOTOSYNTHESIS

1. <u>Carbon dioxide</u> enters the leaf through tiny holes on the underside of the leaf. The holes are called <u>stomata</u>.
2. <u>Oxygen</u> that is produced by photosynthesis leaves through the stomata by <u>diffusion</u>.
3. <u>Chloroplasts</u> are most abundant near the upper surface of the leaf in <u>palisade</u> <u>cells</u>. Chloroplasts contain <u>chlorophyll</u>.
- <u>Chlorophyll</u> is a green pigment that <u>absorbs sunlight</u> energy.
4. Inside the leaf are <u>veins</u>; these are continuous with the stem and roots of the plant.

- The veins contain <u>xylem</u> and <u>phloem</u>.
- <u>Xylem</u> transport <u>water</u> from the roots to the leaves.
- <u>Phloem</u> transport the <u>glucose</u> up and down the plant to where it is needed particularly the growing regions (the bud) and the storage areas (the roots).

FACTORS AFFECTING THE RATE OF PHOTOSYNTHESIS

FACTORS AFFECTING THE RATE OF PHOTOSYNTHESIS	LIGHT	CARBON DIOXIDE	TEMPERATURE
· There are <u>three</u> things that affect the rate of photosynthesis. They are:	· If there is more light then the rate of photosynthesis will increase.	If the carbon dioxide concentration is increased then photosynthesis will increase.	· The best temperature for photosynthesis is about 30°C. · Once you get above 45°C, photosynthesis slows down.

PHOTOSYNTHESIS EXPERIMENTS

iodine

- A plant will store the glucose as <u>starch</u> once it has been made.
- We can test whether the leaf has photo-synthesised or not by testing the leaf for starch.
1. Dip a leaf in boiling water for about a minute to soften it.
2. Put the leaf in a test tube of ethanol and stand in hot water for 10 minutes. (This removes the colour.)
3. Remove and wash the leaf.
4. Lay the leaf flat in a petri dish and add <u>iodine</u>.

5. If starch is present the leaf should go blue/black.

- You can repeat the experiment on a plant that has been kept in the dark for 24 hours or a leaf that has been kept in a flask without carbon dioxide.
- You should find that the iodine stays brown proving that light and carbon dioxide are needed for photosynthesis.

HEALTHY GROWTH

- *Minerals are absorbed from the soil dissolved in water by the roots.*
- *The roots are specially designed to absorb water from the soil.*
- *There are three essential minerals needed for healthy growth:*

1. <u>Nitrates</u> are needed to make proteins.

2. <u>Phosphates</u> play an important role in photosynthesis and in helping the plant use some of its glucose for respiration.

3. <u>Potassium</u> is involved in making the enzymes used in respiration and photosynthesis work.

- *Lack of minerals cause the following mineral deficiency symptoms:*

lack of nitrates causes stunted growth and yellow, older leaves

lack of phosphates causes poor root growth and purple, young leaves

lack of potassium causes yellow leaves with dead spots

QUICK TEST

1. What five things does a plant need for photosynthesis?
2. What does a plant produce in photosynthesis?
3. Where does photosynthesis take place?
4. What do the plants do with the glucose they make?
5. What are the three main minerals a plant needs?

1. Carbon dioxide, water, chlorophyll, light and suitable temperature.
2. Oxygen and glucose
3. The leaf
4. They release energy in respiration, generate other useful substances and store it as starch.
5. Nitrates, phosphates and potassium.

PLANT REPRODUCTION

- Plants have male and female sex cells just like animals.
- They reproduce to form seeds inside fru
- Reproduction consists of pollination, fertilisation, seed dispersal, and germination.

THE FLOWER

- Many flowers contain male and female reproductive organs.
- The male sex cell is called a <u>pollen grain</u>.
- The female sex cell is called an <u>ovule</u>.

Carpel: these are the female parts of the flower and consist of the <u>stigma</u>, which receives the pollen grains, <u>style</u> and <u>ovary</u>. The ovary contains the <u>ovules</u>.

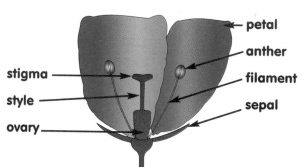

Labels: petal, stigma, style, ovary, anther, filament, sepal

Petal: these are often brightly coloured to attract insects for pollination.

Stamen: these are the male parts of the flower (<u>staMEN</u>) and consist of an <u>anther</u>, which produces the <u>pollen grains</u>, and the <u>filament</u>.

Sepals: these protect the bud. They are green and are just below the flower petals.

POLLINATION

- *This is the beginning of making a seed.*
- *The pollen grain from the anther must be transferred to the stigma; either of the same plant (<u>self-pollination</u>) or the stigma of another plant (<u>cross-pollination</u>).*
- *This can be achieved by <u>wind</u> <u>or</u> <u>by</u> <u>insects</u>.*

Examiner's Top Tip
Learn the differences between plants that use the wind to achieve pollination and the plants that use insects.

INSECT POLLINATION
Insects such as bees carry pollen on their bodies from the anther to the sticky stigmas.
- *Flowers that use insect pollination to reproduce usually:*
- *have brightly coloured petals*
- *have scented flowers*
- *contain sugary nectar inside them.*

Labels: anther, stigma

WIND POLLINATION
Flowers that use wind pollination to reproduce usually have:
- *less brightly coloured petals*
- *no scent*
- *no nectar*
- *filaments that hang the anthers outside the flower to catch the wind.*
They produce more pollen than insect pollinated plants.

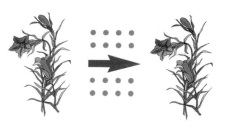

FERTILISATION

- Fertilisation occurs when the male pollen grain joins with a female ovule.
- The <u>pollen nucleus</u> <u>fuses</u> <u>with</u> the <u>ovule nucleus</u>. The ovule nucleus can then grow into a seed.

STEPS

- The pollen grain lands on the stigma with help from insects or the wind.
- A <u>pollen tube</u> grows out of the pollen down the style towards the ovary
- The pollen nucleus moves down the tube to join with the ovule nucleus
- Fertilisation has occurred; the ovary turns into a fruit and inside it the ovule grows into a seed.

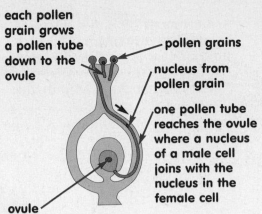

each pollen grain grows a pollen tube down to the ovule

pollen grains

nucleus from pollen grain

one pollen tube reaches the ovule where a nucleus of a male cell joins with the nucleus in the female cell

ovule

SEEDS AND SEED DISPERSAL

- Plants try to scatter their seed over a wide a range as possible so the seed has the opportunity to grow into plants with little competition for resources.
- The scattering of seeds is called <u>dispersal</u>. There are three different methods used by plants.

tough seed coat for protection

embryo root

embryo shoot

food store

WIND DISPERSAL

- The fruits of these plants are light and so are easily picked up by the wind.

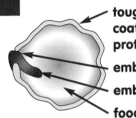

thistle   dandelion

ANIMAL DISPERSAL

- Animals eat the tomato.
- The animals move to another place before producing droppings that contain the seeds.

tomato

POPPING OUT

- These pods dry out and pop open to flick out the seeds.

sweet pea

GERMINATION

- Once settled, the seeds will begin to grow into a new plant – but only if conditions are right.
- The conditions necessary for seeds to germinate are <u>moisture</u>, <u>warmth</u> and <u>enough</u> <u>oxygen</u> in the air.
- The root is sensitive to gravity and the shoot is sensitive to light so they will grow naturally in the right directions.

QUICK TEST

1. What is the female part of the flower called?

2. What is the male part of the flower called?

3. What is the difference between cross-pollination and self-pollination?

4. Name the two ways that pollen can be transferred to a stigma.

5. Name three ways that seeds are dispersed

6. What is fertilisation in plants?

7. What do the ovaries and the ovules become after fertilisation?

8. What are the best conditions for germination?

8. Moisture, warmth and oxygen.
7. Ovaries become fruit, ovules become seeds
6. The joining of a male pollen nucleus with a female ovule nucleus.
5. By animals, popping out of pods and the wind
4. By insects or the wind.
3. Cross-pollination is between two different plants; self-pollination is when the plant pollinates itself.
2. Stamen
1. Carpel

THE CARBON CYCLE

- Carbon dioxide and nitrogen are <u>atmospheric</u> <u>gases</u>.
- These amounts should stay the same, as they are constantly recycled in the environment.

PHOTOSYNTHESIS

Plants absorb carbon dioxide from the air. They use the carbon to make carbohydrates, proteins and fats using the <u>Sun</u> as an energy source.

FEEDING

Animals eat plants and so the carbon gets into their bodies.

RESPIRATION

- Plants, animals and decomposers carry out respiration and release carbon dioxide into the air.

DEATH AND DECAY

Plants and animals die and produce waste. The carbon is released into the soil.

BURNING AND COMBUSTION

The burning of fossil fuels (coal, oil and gas) releases carbon dioxide into the atmosphere.

DECOMPOSERS

Bacteria and fungi present in the soil break down dead matter, urine and faeces, which contain carbon. Bacteria and fungi release carbon dioxide when they respire.

Examiner's Top Tip
The carbon cycle in the exam may look slightly different, so make sure you learn the processes involved.

FOSSIL FUELS

Coal is formed from plants; oil and gas are formed from animals.

DEATH BUT NO DECAY

Sometimes plants and animals die, but do not decay. Heat and pressure gradually, over millions of years, produce fossil fuels.

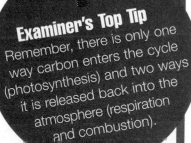

Examiner's Top Tip
Remember, there is only one way carbon enters the cycle (photosynthesis) and two ways it is released back into the atmosphere (respiration and combustion).

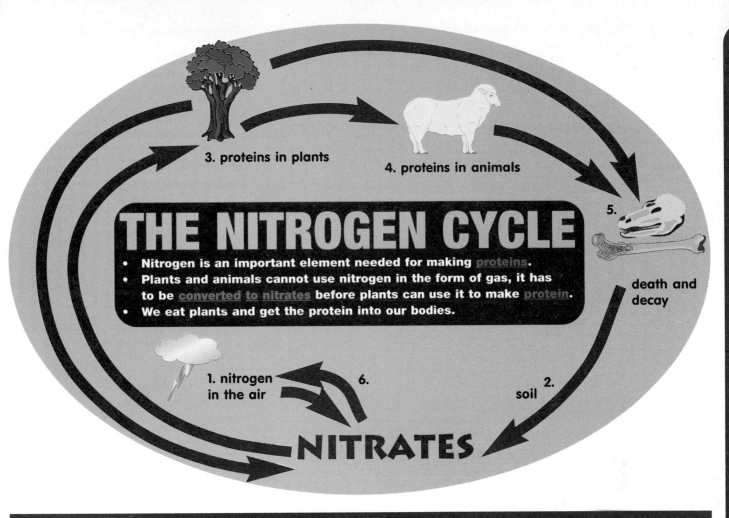

3. proteins in plants

4. proteins in animals

5.

death and decay

THE NITROGEN CYCLE

- Nitrogen is an important element needed for making proteins.
- Plants and animals cannot use nitrogen in the form of gas, it has to be converted to nitrates before plants can use it to make protein.
- We eat plants and get the protein into our bodies.

1. nitrogen in the air

6.

2. soil

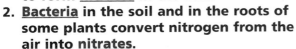

NITRATES

NITROGEN GAS IS CHANGED INTO NITRATES IN THE NITROGEN CYCLE

Nitrogen gas in the air
1. Lightning – causes nitrogen and oxygen to combine to form nitrogen oxides. These dissolve in rain and are washed into the soil to form nitrates in the soil.

lightning

2. Bacteria in the soil and in the roots of some plants convert nitrogen from the air into nitrates.
3. Plants take up the nitrates from the soil and convert them into proteins.
4. Animals eat the plants, take the protein into their bodies and it becomes part of its protein.

5. Animals and plants produce waste and eventually die and decay releasing the nitrates back into the soil.
6. Nitrates can be washed out of the soil before plants take them up. Denitrifying bacteria live in waterlogged soils; they can change nitrates into nitrogen gas that is returned to the atmosphere.

denitrifying bacteria in waterlogged soil

QUICK TEST

1. Name the process that absorbs carbon dioxide from the air.
2. What are the two ways that carbon is released back into the air?
3. What happens to the bodies of animals and plants that do not decay?
4. What do plants need nitrogen for?
5. What does nitrogen have to be converted to before it is used?

1. Photosynthesis.
2. Respiration and burning/combustion.
3. Turned into fossil fuels.
4. For making proteins.
5. Nitrates

CLASSIFICATION

- Classification is what scientists use to sort out all living organisms into groups.
- The organisms are put into groups according to the <u>similarities</u> between them.
- All living things are divided first into <u>kingdoms</u>.
- The <u>two main kingdoms</u> are the <u>animal</u> and <u>plant</u> kingdoms.

THE ANIMAL KINGDOM

- Animals can be divided up into two groups, the <u>vertebrates</u> and the <u>invertebrates</u>.
- <u>Vertebrates</u> are animals <u>with</u> <u>a</u> <u>backbone</u>.
- <u>Invertebrates</u> are animals <u>without</u> <u>a</u> <u>backbone</u>.

VERTEBRATES

vertebrates (animals with backbones)

| fish | mammals | amphibians | reptiles | birds |

Vertebrates are divided into five groups and each of the groups has features that are specific only to them:
- <u>Fish</u> These live in water, have fins and scales, breathe through gills.
- <u>Mammals</u> These have hair on their bodies, are warm-blooded, give birth to live young and feed their young on milk from the mother.
- <u>Amphibians</u> These have smooth moist skin, live on water and land, but breed in water.
- <u>Reptiles</u> These have dry, scaly skin and most live on land
- <u>Birds</u> These have feathers and wings, most can fly and they lay eggs.

INVERTEBRATES

invertebrates (animals without backbones)

| cnidarians sac-like body with tentacles | flatworms flat body with mouth at one end | roundworms long, thread-like body | segmented worms body divided into segments | molluscs have a shell and a muscular 'root' | echinoderms spiny skins and a pattern of five parts |

- The <u>invertebrates</u> are divided into groups and each of these groups has features specific only to them.
- Another <u>invertebrate</u> group are the anthropods; they have jointed legs and hard outer skeletons.
- They can be subdivided into four other groups.

arthropods

| arachnids body in two parts four pairs of legs | crustaceans hard, outer skeleton | insects three parts to body three pairs of legs two pairs of wings | centipedes many pairs of legs |

THE PLANT KINGDOM

Plants can be classified into the following groups:

plants

| mosses and liverworts
no proper roots or stems
thin leaves that lose water
make spores | ferns
strong stems, roots
and leaves
make spores | conifers
needle-like leaves
seeds made inside cones | flowering plants
have flowers which
make seeds |

USING KEYS

- To help people <u>identify</u> living things we can use <u>keys</u>.
- Keys are a series of questions that have <u>two</u> <u>possible</u> <u>answers</u>.
- Eventually the questions divide the group until there is only one option.
- The option left will be the identification of the plant or animal.
- There are two main types of key.

TYPE 1

- Choose one organism for example (A), to try to identify and go to the start.
- Answer the first question: Has it got legs?
- The answer is no, so follow the 'no' arrow.
- Answer the next question: Has it got a shell?
- The answer is yes, so follow the 'yes' arrow. You can't go any further, so the answer is a snail.
- Go back to the start and choose another animal to identify.

TYPE 2

- We can use a different type of key to identify the animals above.
- Again choose an organism for example (E)
- Answer the first question for that organism and follow the instructions that follow
1. Does it have a shell? ... No, go to 2 ...Yes, it's a snail
2. Does it have legs? ...No, it's a worm ...Yes, go to 3
3. Does it have more than four pairs of legs? ...No, go to 4 ...Yes, it's a centipede
4. Does it have wings? ...No, it's a spider ...Yes, it's a damsel fly.
- Did you find out that organism (E) was a worm?

Start
Has it got legs?
yes — Has it got wings?
no — Has it got a shell?
yes — Damsel fly larva
no — Does it have more than four pairs of legs?
yes — Centipede
no — Spider
yes — Snail
no — Worm

QUICK TEST

1. **What is classification?**

2. **What does invertebrate mean?**

3. **What does vertebrate mean?**

4. **Can you name the vertebrate groups?**

5. **Using the keys section, go back and identify the rest of the animals.**

VaRIATiON

- All living things vary in the way they look or behave.
- Living things that belong to the same species are all slightly different.
- Living things that belong to different species are totally different.
- Inheritance, the environment or a combination of both may cause these differences.

GENETIC VARIATION

- Why do we look like we do? The answer is because we have inherited our characteristics from our parents.
- Brothers and sisters are not exactly the same as each other because they inherit different genes from their parents. It is completely random.
- Only identical twins have the same genes.
- Genes are made up of a chemical called DNA and are found on the chromosomes.
- Genes occur in pairs and control all our inherited characteristics.
- Chromosomes are found in the nucleus of all our cells.
- Human body cells have 46 chromosomes (23 pairs).
- Sperm and egg cells have 23 chromosomes.
- When they fuse together during fertilisation the fertilised egg has 46 chromosomes with all the information to grow into a baby.

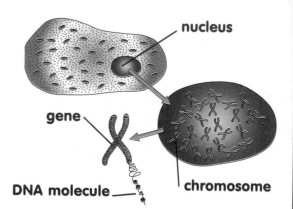

nucleus

gene

DNA molecule

chromosome

ENVIRONMENTAL VARIATION

- The environment is your surroundings and all the things that may affect your upbringing.
- Identical twins may be separated at birth and grow up in totally different surroundings, following different diets for example.
- Any differences between the twins must be due to the environment they were brought up in as they have identical genes.
- Many of the differences between people are caused by a combination of genetic and environmental influences.

VARIATION IN PLANTS

- Plants inherit characteristics by their genes in the same way as animals do.
- However, plants are affected more than animals by small changes in the environment.
- Sunlight, temperature, moisture level and soil type are factors that will determine how well a plant grows.
- A plant grown in sunlight will grow much faster and may double in size compared to a plant grown in the shade, whereas an animal would not be affected.

VARIATION IN ANIMALS

- We vary because of the random way our genes are <u>inherited</u>.
- The environment can affect most of our characteristics. It is usually a combination of genetics and environment that determines how we look and behave.
- Just how significant the environment is in determining our features is difficult to assess; for example, is being good at sport inherited or is it due to your upbringing?
- There are some characteristics that are not affected by the environment at all:

1. Eye colour   2. Natural hair colour   3. Blood group   4. Inherited diseases

CONTINUOUS AND DISCONTINUOUS VARIATION

- Differences between animals and plants show two types of variation.
- If you measured the heights of people in your class you would find that they varied gradually from short to tall.
- <u>Height</u> <u>or</u> <u>weight</u> <u>follows</u> <u>continuous</u> <u>variation</u>.

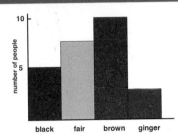

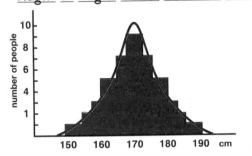

- If you looked at the hair colour of people in your class, you would find there are only a few options, not a continuous range.
- Another example is whether a person can roll their tongue. You either can or you cannot; there is no in between.
- <u>Eye</u> <u>colour</u>, <u>hair</u> <u>colour</u>, <u>blood</u> <u>group</u> and <u>rolling</u> <u>tongues</u> <u>are</u> <u>examples</u> <u>of</u> <u>discontinuous</u> <u>variation</u>.

SELECTIVE BREEDING

Selective breeding is where features that are wanted in a plant or animal are bred in and features that are not wanted are bred out. This is done by:

- Selecting the individuals with the <u>best</u> <u>characteristics</u> and breeding from them.
- Some of the offspring will have inherited some of the best features; the best offspring are selected and are bred together.
- This is repeated over generations until the <u>new</u> <u>varieties</u> have all the desired characteristics.
- Humans carry out selective breeding to benefit themselves in some way.

Examples include:
- Developing plants that are <u>resistant</u> <u>to</u> <u>disease</u> <u>or</u> <u>frost</u>, or fruit that tastes good.
- Breeding dogs for their <u>intelligence</u> or for <u>showing</u>.
- Breeding cows to produce <u>more</u> <u>milk</u> or <u>better</u> <u>tasting</u> <u>beef</u>.
- Breeding racehorses that can <u>run</u> <u>fast</u>.

small and tasty

large but tasteless

large but tasty

Examiner's Top Tip
Learn examples of continuous and discontinuous variation.

QUICK TEST

1. Is blood group inherited or caused by the environment?
2. Is having a scar environmental or inherited?
3. Give two examples of continuous variation.
4. Give two examples of discontinuous variation.
5. What is selective breeding?

5. Breeding animals and plants together to produce the best offspring.
4. Eye colour, blood group, hair colour, tongue rolling (any two).
3. Height and weight
2. Environmental
1. Inherited

FOOD CHAINS

- The <u>arrows</u> in a food chain show the transfer of food energy from organism to organism.
- <u>Food chains always begin with the Sun, then a green plant</u>; these can include seeds, fruits or even dead leaves.

<u>Producers</u> – green plants use the Sun's energy to produce food energy.

<u>Consumers</u> – animals that get their energy from eating other living things.

<u>Primary consumers</u> – animals that eat the producers.

<u>Secondary consumers</u> – animals that eat the primary consumers.

<u>Tertiary consumers</u> – animals that eat the secondary consumers.

<u>Herbivores</u> – animals that only eat plants.

<u>Carnivores</u> – animals that only eat animals.

<u>Top carnivores</u> – animals that are not eaten by anything else except decomposers after they die.

LOSS OF ENERGY IN FOOD CHAINS

- Food chains rarely have more than four or five links in them; this is because energy is lost along the way.
- The energy is used up for staying alive, moving, growing and keeping warm, and some of the energy is lost as waste in urine and faeces.
- Not all of the animal material is eaten so not all of the energy is passed on.
- This loss of energy in a food chain means that the numbers of organisms gets less at each level.

FOOD WEBS

- A food web gives us a more complete picture of who eats what.
- Most animals in a community eat more than one thing. If one kind of food runs out, they will be able to survive by eating something else.
- <u>Food webs are made up of many food chains linked together</u>.
- Food chains can be drawn for any environment.

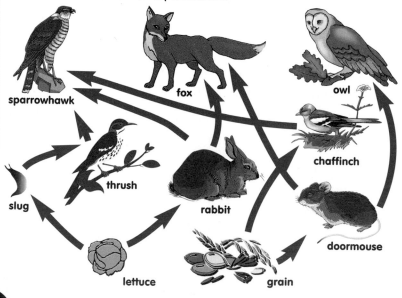

sparrowhawk   fox   owl

thrush   chaffinch

slug   rabbit   doormouse

lettuce   grain

POISONS IN FOOD CHAINS

- Poisons can get into food chains with devastating consequences, especially for the top carnivore.
- An example of this is a pesticide called DDT that got into food chains. Fortunately, this is no longer used.
- As DDT passes up the food chain it becomes more concentrated.

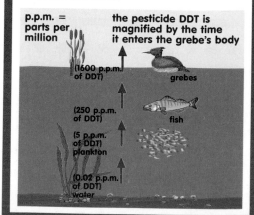

p.p.m. = parts per million

the pesticide DDT is magnified by the time it enters the grebe's body

(1600 p.p.m. of DDT)   grebes

(250 p.p.m. of DDT)   fish

(5 p.p.m. of DDT) plankton

(0.02 p.p.m. of DDT) water

PYRAMIDS OF NUMBERS

- If we look at the information a food chain tells us, it is simply who eats who.
- A pyramid if numbers tells us how many organisms are involved at each stage in the food chain.
- Sometimes a pyramid of numbers doesn't look like a pyramid at all as it doesn't take into account the <u>size</u> of the organisms
- A rosebush is one organism but it has many leaves to support many aphids.

fox
rabbit
grass

blackbird
ladybirds
aphids
rosebush

PYRAMIDS OF BIOMASS

blackbird
ladybirds
aphids
rosebush

- A biomass pyramid takes into account the <u>size of an organism</u> at each level.
- It looks at the <u>mass of each organism</u>.
- A single rosebush weighs more than the aphids and lots of aphids weigh more than the few ladybirds that feed on them.

FOOD CHAINS AND WEBS

- Food chains and webs <u>begin with energy from the Sun</u>.
- A <u>food chain</u> shows us what eats what in a community.
- A <u>food web</u> is made up of interconnected food chains.

grass   rabbit   fox

TYPICAL EXAM QUESTIONS

Exam questions often focus on what would happen to a food web if an animal was removed by disease or other factors.
- In the food web (left) what would happen if the rabbits were removed?
- Look at who would get eaten due to less competition.
- Who would increase in number due to not being eaten?
- Who would go hungry due to their food source being removed?
- What effect would removing an organism have on the other animals and plants in the food web?

QUICK TEST

1. What is a producer?
2. What is a consumer?
3. Where does the energy come from that begins a food chain?
4. What do pyramids of numbers show?
5. What do pyramids of biomass take into account?

1. A plant that produces food from the Sun's energy.
2. An animal that eats other plants and animals.
3. The Sun
4. The numbers of organisms involved in a food chain.
5. The mass of organisms involved in a food chain.

ADAPTATION AND COMPETITION

- A <u>habitat</u> is where an organism lives; it has the conditions needed for it to survive.
- A <u>community</u> consists of living things in the <u>habitat</u>.
- Each <u>community</u> is made up of different <u>populations</u> of <u>animals</u> and <u>plants</u>.
- Each <u>population</u> is adapted to live in that particular habitat.

SIZES OF POPULATIONS

Population numbers cannot keep growing out of control; factors that keep the population from becoming too large are called <u>limiting</u> <u>factors</u>. The factors that affect the size of a population are:

- amount of food and water available
- predators or grazing – who may eat the animal or plant
- disease
- climate, temperature, floods, droughts and storms
- competition for space, mates, light, food and water
- human activity such as pollution or destruction of habitats.

Organisms will only live and reproduce where conditions are suitable; the amount of light, the temperature and the availability of food and water will affect the organisms and are essential for their survival. These factors vary with time of day and time of year; this helps explain why organisms vary from place to place, and are restricted to certain habitats. Organisms have adapted to live in certain areas.

ADAPTATION

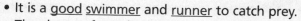

You never see a polar bear in the desert or a camel at the North Pole. This is because they have not <u>adapted</u> to live there. They have adapted to live where they do; they have <u>special</u> <u>features</u> that help them survive.

A polar bear lives in cold, arctic regions of the world; it has many features that enable it to survive:

- It has a <u>thick</u> <u>coat</u> to keep in body heat, as well as a <u>layer</u> <u>of</u> <u>blubber</u> for insulation.
- Its coat is <u>white</u> so that it can blend into its surroundings.
- Its <u>fur</u> <u>is</u> <u>greasy</u> so that it doesn't hold water after swimming. This prevents cooling by evaporation.
- A polar bear has <u>big</u> <u>feet</u> to spread its weight on snow and ice; it also has big, <u>sharp</u> <u>claws</u> to catch fish.

- It is a <u>good</u> <u>swimmer</u> and <u>runner</u> to catch prey.
- The shape of a polar bear is <u>compact</u> even though it is large. This keeps the surface area to a minimum to reduce loss of body heat.

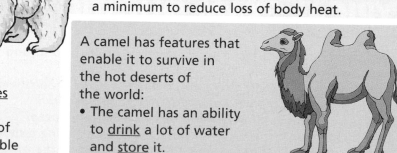

A camel has features that enable it to survive in the hot deserts of the world:

- The camel has an ability to <u>drink</u> a lot of water and <u>store</u> it.
- It loses very little water as it produces <u>little</u> <u>urine</u> and it can cope with big changes in temperature, so there <u>is</u> <u>no</u> <u>need</u> <u>for</u> <u>sweating</u>.
- All fat is stored in the humps, so there is <u>no insulation layer</u>.
- Its <u>sandy</u> colour provides <u>camouflage</u>.
- It has a <u>large surface area</u> to enable it to lose heat.

In a community, the animal or plant best adapted to its surroundings will survive.

COMPETITION

- As the populations grow, there may be overcrowding and limited resources to support the growing numbers.
- Populations cannot keep growing out of control.
- Animals have to compete for <u>space, food</u> and <u>water</u> in their struggle to survive.
- Only the strongest will survive leading to the <u>survival</u> of <u>the</u> <u>fittest</u>.
- Plants compete for <u>space</u>, <u>light</u>, <u>water</u> and <u>nutrients</u>.
- If an animal or a plant can adapt to its environment then it will survive and breed.

PREDATOR/PREY GRAPHS

- **In a community, the number of animals stays fairly constant; this is partly due to the amount of food limiting the size of the populations.**
- **A <u>predator</u> is an animal which hunts and kills another animal.**
- **The <u>prey</u> is the hunted animal.**
- **Populations of predator and prey go in cycles.**
- **Follow the graph to see how the numbers of prey affect the numbers of predators and vice versa.**

predator

prey

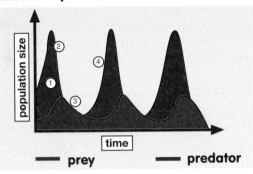

1. If the population of prey increases, there is more food for the predator, so its numbers increase.
2. This causes the number of prey to decrease as they are eaten.
3. This causes the number of predators to decrease, as there is not enough food.
4. If the predator numbers fall, the prey numbers can increase again, as they are not being eaten, and so on.

- **<u>Predators</u> <u>have</u> <u>adapted</u> to survive by being strong, agile and fast. They have good vision and a camouflaged body. They also tend to hunt in packs, have a variety of prey, and often hunt the young, sick and old.**
- **<u>Prey</u> <u>have</u> <u>also</u> <u>adapted</u>; the best adapted escape and breed.**
- **Adaptations of prey include: being able to run, swim and fly fast; they stay in large groups; they have a horrible taste; warning colours and camouflage.**

SURVIVAL

- The amount of light, temperature and availability of food and water will affect the organism and are essential for its survival.
- These factors vary in time of day and year.

DAILY ADAPTATIONS INCLUDE:
- plants closing their flowers at night for protection
- animals that are nocturnal and sleep during the day to avoid predators.

YEARLY ADAPTATIONS INCLUDE:
- animals hibernating, growing thick coats, migrating to warmer areas and storing food
- plants losing their leaves in winter and flowers dying off as there are less birds or insects to pollinate them.

QUICK TEST

1. What is a habitat?
2. What things do animals compete for?
3. What things do plants compete for?
4. Why do the numbers of prey and predators in a community stay fairly constant?
5. What factor determines whether animals or plants survive in their environments?

5. Only the best-adapted organism will survive.
4. Because of the predator-prey cycle
3. Light, space, water and nutrients.
2. Food, water, and space.
1. Where an organism lives.

EXAM QUESTIONS — Use the questions to test your progress. Check your answers on page 124.

1. Identify the labels a) b) and c) of this animal cell

a) ....

b) ....

c) ....

2. Which part of the plant cell absorbs the Sun's energy for photosynthesis?

....

3. What type of cell is this and what does it do?

....

....

4. Match each cell with its function:

    1. white blood cell   a) absorbs water from the soil

    2. ciliated cell   b) fights disease

    3. nerve cell   c) carries messages

    4. Root hair cell   d) carries mucus

5. Name the five parts that make up the plant..

6. Which human organ system is responsible for transporting blood around the body?.......................

7. Where are the male and female sex cells in the flower?.....................................

8. Finish this word equation for photosynthesis

Light

carbon dioxide + a)_____   ➡   glucose + c)_____

                  b) _____

9. Which group of vertebrates have dry, scaly skin and mostly live on land?.............................

10. What happens to food in the stomach?.......................................

11. Where is the information stored that controls your characteristics?...............................

12. What is the name of the process where digested food passes into the blood stream?

....

13. State three reasons why the villi on the surface of the small intestine are good for absorption.

....

14. Put this food chain in the correct order:

    snail   blackbird   oak-tree leaves

....

15. Name three diseases associated with smoking..

16. Complete the equation for respiration:

    Glucose + a)................ ➡ Carbon dioxide + b)................ + c)................

17. What four parts make up the human blood?..

18. What are the differences between an artery and a vein?...
....

19. Explain three ways in which white blood cells fight disease causing microbes......................
....

20. List as many ways as you can in which the baby is protected in the womb...........................
....

21. What are antagonistic muscles? Give an example..

22. Replace the letters a–f on the diagram of the breathing system below.
a) .... b) .... c) .... d) .... e) .... f) ....

23. What is natural immunity?..

24. Which three minerals are needed for healthy growth in a plant?.....................................

25. What is carpel and what does it consist of?...
....

26. What is the name of the process which farmers use to improve their crops or livestock?..................

27. List the ways in which the air we breathe in is different to the air we breathe out.
....

28. How many chromosomes does a human body cell have?..

29. What is pollination?..

30. Name the seven food groups that make up a balanced diet...
....

How did you do?

1–8	correct	....start again
9–16	correct	....getting there
17–24	correct	....good work
25–30	correct	

43

IGNEOUS ROCKS

- All **igneous** **rocks** are formed from **molten** **rock** which has **cooled** and **solidified**. Molten rock below the surface of the Earth is called magma, above the Earth's surface it is called lava.

- **Igneous** **rocks** are very hard and have **crystals**.

- **Extrusive** **igneous** **rocks** have **small** **crystals** because they have formed very quickly above ground. Basalt is an example of an extrusive igneous rock.

- **Intrusive** **igneous** **rocks** have **large** **crystals** because they solidified slowly below the ground. Granite is an example of an intrusive igneous rock.

granite has large crystals

Examiner's Top Tip
There are quite a lot of facts here – make a table with these headings: rock type, characteristics, formation and examples, and include all the information in the table.

SEDIMENTARY ROCKS

- *Sedimentary* *rocks* tend to be *crumbly* and sometimes contain *fossils*. Sandstone and limestone are examples of sedimentary rocks.

sandstone

limestone

- *Sedimentary* *rocks* form from *layers* *of* *sediment* found in seas or lakes. Over millions of years these layers are buried by further sediment. The weight of these layers *squeezes* *out* *the* *water* and the *particles* *become* *cemented* *together*.

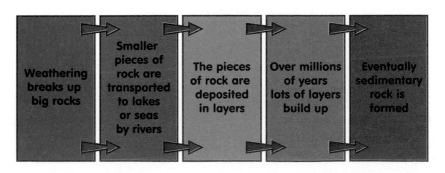

| Weathering breaks up big rocks | Smaller pieces of rock are transported to lakes or seas by rivers | The pieces of rock are deposited in layers | Over millions of years lots of layers build up | Eventually sedimentary rock is formed |

If you are very lucky you might find a fossil in a sedimentary rock.

METAMORPHIC ROCKS

schist (schist and gneiss are examples of metamorphic rocks)

Metamorphic <u>rocks</u> are usually <u>hard</u> and may contain <u>banded crystals</u>. Metamorphic rocks are formed by <u>high temperature</u> and <u>pressure</u> on existing rocks. Metamorphic rocks are created when:

- rock is <u>stressed</u> as mountains are formed
- <u>hot magma</u> comes into contact with rock causing alteration of the existing rocks.

ROCKS CAN BE CLASSIFIED INTO 3 GROUPS:
IGNEOUS, SEDIMENTARY AND METAMORPHIC ROCKS

QUICK TEST

1. Which type of rock is formed when molten rock cools and solidifies?
2. Which type of rock is the hardest?
3. Which sort of igneous rock has small crystals and was formed quickly?
4. Which sort of igneous rock has large crystals and was formed slowly?
5. Give two examples of igneous rocks.
6. Which type of rock may contain fossils?
7. Over what sort of time period do sedimentary rocks form?
8. Give two examples of sedimentary rocks.
9. What two factors can cause existing rock to be changed into metamorphic rock?
10. Give two examples of metamorphic rocks.

10. Schist, gneiss
9. Heat, pressure
8. Sandstone, limestone
7. Millions of years
6. Sedimentary
5. Basalt and granite
4. Intrusive e.g. granite
3. Extrusive e.g. basalt
2. Igneous
1. Igneous

WEATHERING

Weathering is the breaking down of larger rocks into smaller pieces. There are two important ways in which rocks at the Earth's surface are weathered. These are: physical weathering and chemical weathering.

PHYSICAL WEATHERING

This happens when rocks are subjected to changes in temperature.

FREEZE THAW

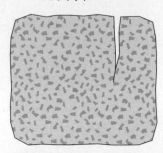 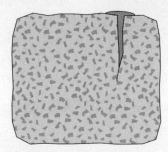 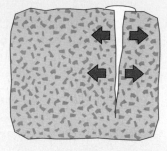

a rock with a small crack

the crack fills with water

the water freezes and expands, widening the crack

- This type of weathering involves <u>water</u>.
- Water is <u>unusual</u> in that it <u>expands</u> <u>when</u> <u>it</u> <u>freezes</u> (most liquids <u>contract</u> on freezing).
- Water enters into a crack in the rock. When this water freezes it expands and gradually forces the crack in the rock <u>wider</u> <u>apart</u>. This type of weathering is worst in areas where the temperature often varies between just above and just below zero, as the water freezes and thaws more often, so causing more damage.

EFFECT OF THE SUN

- This type of weathering again involves <u>changes</u> <u>in</u> <u>temperature</u>. Rocks are <u>very</u> <u>poor</u> <u>conductors</u> <u>of</u> <u>thermal</u> <u>energy</u>. During the day the rock is gradually warmed up by the heat of the Sun, and the outer layer of the rock expands slightly. At night the temperature drops and the outside of the rock tries to contract, but cannot. Eventually the rock will be broken down.
- This type of weathering is worst in areas where there is a big variation between day and night temperatures.

CHEMICAL WEATHERING

This type of weathering involves a <u>chemical</u> <u>reaction</u>.
Chemical weathering damages <u>statues</u>, <u>buildings</u> and <u>gravestones</u>. It is worst in areas of <u>high</u> <u>pollution</u>.
As rain falls from the sky <u>carbon</u> <u>dioxide</u> in the air dissolves in the rain to form a <u>weak</u> <u>acid</u> which attacks rocks containing calcium carbonate; these rocks include <u>limestone</u>, <u>chalk</u> and <u>marble</u>.
In polluted areas other gases – including <u>sulphur</u> <u>dioxide</u> – also dissolve in the rain water, making it even more <u>acidic</u>.

THE ROCK CYCLE

Rocks are continually being **broken down** and then **built up** again. During the rock cycle, **one type of rock is changed into another**.

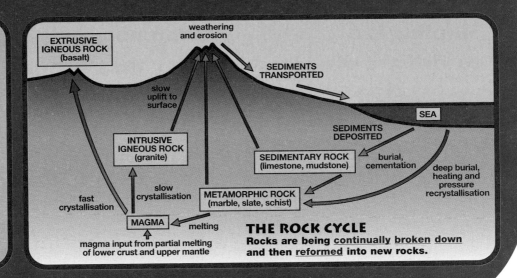

THE ROCK CYCLE
Rocks are being <u>continually</u> <u>broken</u> <u>down</u> and then <u>reformed</u> into new rocks.

STAGES OF THE ROCK CYCLE

- During <u>weathering</u> large rocks are broken down into <u>smaller pieces</u>.
- <u>Erosion</u> is the wearing down of rock.
- Transportation is the movement of the eroded pieces of rock, usually by rivers and streams in this country, but also by wind and glaciers.
- <u>Deposition</u> occurs when sediment is laid down as the river can no longer carry it along.

QUICK TEST

1. What is weathering?
2. What is involved in all types of physical weathering?
3. Which substance is involved in freeze-thaw weathering?
4. What happens during freeze-thaw weathering?
5. What effect does the Sun have on rocks?
6. Which gas is dissolved in all rain water and makes it weakly acidic?
7. Why is chemical weathering worst in polluted areas?
8. What is transportation?
9. What normally carries the eroded rock pieces during transportation?
10. In which process are the pieces of rock laid down as sediment?

Examiner's Top Tip
The rock cycle involves the same particles being reused over and over again. These processes happen over very long periods of time.

10. Deposition
9. Water/wind/glaciers
8. The movement of eroded rock pieces.
7. Other gases, including sulphur dioxide, dissolve in the rain water.
6. Carbon dioxide
5. Rock expands during the day then tries to contract at night, and is cracked open.
4. Water freezes and expands in existing cracks, breaking rocks apart.
3. Water
2. Changes in temperature.
1. The breaking down of larger rocks to smaller pieces.

ACID RAIN

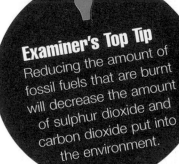

- Fossil fuels may contain some <u>sulphur</u>.
- Sulphur is a <u>non-metal</u>. When non-metal oxides are dissolved in water they form <u>acidic</u> <u>solutions</u>.
- When these fuels are burnt sulphur dioxide is produced and released into the atmosphere.
- This gas dissolves in rain water to produce acid rain.
- This acid rain can harm statues and buildings which are made of rock that contains calcium carbonate, like <u>limestone</u>, <u>chalk</u> and <u>marble</u>.
- Acid rain can also attack exposed metals.
- Acid rain can damage – and even kill – trees. It can also harm animals and plants.

Examiner's Top Tip
Reducing the amount of fossil fuels that are burnt will decrease the amount of sulphur dioxide and carbon dioxide put into the environment.

CARBON DIOXIDE AND THE GREENHOUSE EFFECT

- The <u>greenhouse effect</u> is slowly heating up the Earth.
- When fossil fuels are burnt <u>carbon dioxide</u> is produced.
- Although some of this carbon dioxide is removed from the atmosphere when the gas dissolves in the oceans, the overall amount of carbon dioxide in the atmosphere has <u>gradually increased</u> over the last 200 years.
- This carbon dioxide <u>traps the heat</u> that has reached the Earth from the Sun.
- Global warming may mean that the ice at the North and South Poles will melt and cause massive flooding.

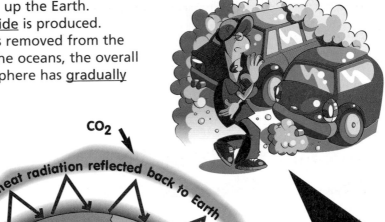

CO$_2$

heat radiation reflected back to Earth

light energy from the sun

Examiner's Top Tip
The greenhouse effect is caused by carbon dioxide.

POLLUTION OF THE ATMOSPHERE

The atmosphere is being polluted in many ways.

QUICK TEST

1. What is formed when the sulphur in fossil fuels is burnt?
2. What does this form when it dissolves in rain water?
3. What environmental problems can this cause?
4. Which rock(s) does acid rain attack?
5. Which gas is responsible for global warming?
6. Why are the amounts of carbon dioxide in the environment increasing?
7. Where does some of the carbon dioxide go?
8. What does the carbon dioxide do?
9. What could be the effect of global warming on the environment?
10. Why would this be a problem?

Examiner's Top Tip
Acid rain is caused by sulphur dioxide.

10. We need land to live and grow food on.
9. Massive flooding
8. Causes a gradual increase in temperature on Earth.
7. It dissolves in oceans.
6. Because fossil fuels are being burnt.
5. Carbon dioxide
4. Limestone/chalk/marble
3. It can damage statues and buildings, trees, animals and plants.
2. acid rain
1. Sulphur dioxide

SOLIDS

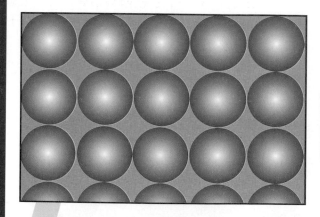

- particles <u>are</u> <u>very</u> <u>close</u> <u>together</u>
- <u>particles</u> are <u>held</u> <u>together</u> by <u>strong</u> <u>forces</u> <u>of</u> <u>attraction</u>
- <u>particles</u> <u>vibrate</u> but have <u>fixed</u> <u>positions</u>

KEY POINT
➡ Solids have a <u>definite</u> <u>shape</u> and <u>volume</u> and are <u>hard</u> <u>to</u> <u>compress</u>.

STATES OF MATTER

THERE ARE ❸ <u>STATES</u> <u>OF</u> <u>MATTER</u>: <u>SOLID</u>, <u>LIQUID</u> AND <u>GAS</u>.

LIQUIDS

- <u>particles</u> are <u>close</u> <u>together</u>
- <u>particles</u> are <u>held</u> <u>together</u> by <u>forces</u> <u>of</u> <u>attraction</u>
- <u>particles</u> <u>move</u> <u>relative</u> to each other

KEY POINT
➡ **Liquids have a <u>definite</u> <u>volume</u>, but <u>not</u> a definite shape and are <u>hard</u> <u>to</u> <u>compress</u>.**

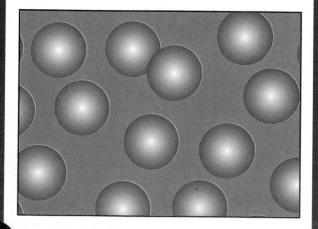

GASES

- <u>particles</u> are <u>far</u> <u>apart</u> from each other
- there are <u>no</u> <u>forces</u> <u>of</u> <u>attraction</u> between particles
- <u>particles</u> <u>move</u> relative to each other

KEY POINT
➡ <u>Gases</u> do <u>not</u> have a <u>definite</u> <u>shape</u> or <u>volume</u> and are <u>easy</u> <u>to</u> <u>compress</u>.

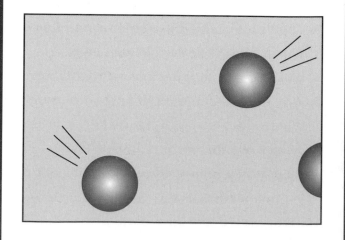

CHANGES OF STATE

When changing from one state to another there is no change in mass.

solid (ice) → liquid (water)

MELTING AND BOILING POINTS

- Above its boiling point a substance is a <u>gas</u>.
- Between its melting point and its boiling point a substance is a <u>liquid</u>.
- Below its melting point a substance is a <u>solid</u>.

- At 25°C (room temperature) <u>oxygen</u> is a <u>gas</u>.
  25°C is above the boiling point of oxygen.
- At 25°C <u>mercury</u> is a <u>liquid</u>.
  25°C is above the melting point but below the boiling point of mercury.
- At 25°C <u>iron</u> is a <u>solid</u>.
  25°C is below the melting point of iron.

substance	melting point °C	boiling point °C
iron	1535	2750
mercury	−39	357
oxygen	−218	−183

CHANGING STATES

a) The particles of the solid are heated and vibrate more.

b) The vibration of the particles overcomes the forces of attraction between the particles.

c) The particles of the liquid are heated and move more quickly.

d) The movement of the liquid particles overcomes the forces of attraction between the particles.

e) The particles in the gas move faster.

temperature increases

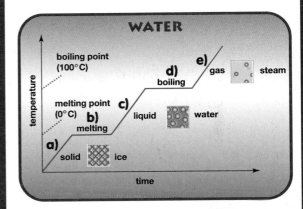

Examiner's Top Tip

This is quite basic stuff so make sure you are really familiar with it. Now draw a temperature time graph to show steam condensing to form liquid water.

QUICK TEST

1. Name the three states of matter.
2. In which of the states are the particles closest together?
3. Do solids have a definite volume?
4. In which state are particles held together by forces of attraction, but the particles may move relative to each other?
5. Can liquids be compressed?
6. Are there any forces of attraction between gas particles?
7. Can gases be compressed easily?
8. In which process do liquids turn into gases?
9. In which process do solids turn into liquids?
10. Draw a temperature time graph to show solid ice melting to form liquid water.

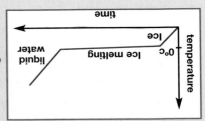

10. See below
9. Melting
8. boiling
7. Yes
6. No
5. No
4. Liquid
3. Yes
2. Solid
1. Solid, liquid and gas

HOW SOLUBLE?

- If a substance <u>dissolves</u> <u>well</u> in a solvent it has a <u>high</u> <u>solubility</u>. To measure <u>how</u> <u>soluble</u> a particular substance is we can find how many grams of it will dissolve in a particular solvent.

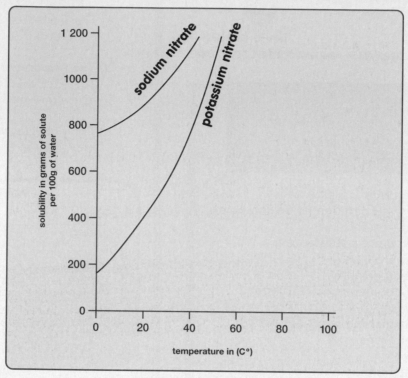

- The graph shows how the solubility of two solutes, sodium nitrate and potassium nitrate, changes as the temperature increases.
- Both of them become more soluble as the temperature rises.
- If no more solute can dissolve in a solvent it is known as a <u>saturated</u> <u>solution</u> (at that temperature).
- Temperature can affect solubility.
- Normally, the <u>higher</u> the temperature the <u>more</u> <u>soluble</u> the substance becomes.
- Temperature can also affect <u>how</u> <u>quickly</u> something dissolves.
- At a higher temperature the particles are moving faster, so the substance will dissolve faster.
- Sugar will dissolve faster in hot water than cold water.

a hot cup of coffee can dissolve more sugar

SOLVENTS AND SOLUTIONS

- Once a solid has dissolved, the <u>liquid</u> (often water) is called the <u>solvent</u>.
- The solid is then called the <u>solute</u>.

  solute + solvent ⇨ solution

- If a substance dissolves in the solvent it is <u>soluble</u>.
- If a substance <u>cannot</u> dissolve in the solvent it is <u>insoluble</u>.
- The insoluble substance may dissolve in a <u>different</u> <u>solvent</u>.

DISSOLVING

- **If a solid dissolves in a liquid it forms a solution.**
- **However, the overall mass stays the same.**

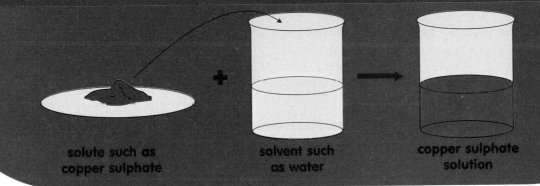

solute such as copper sulphate + solvent such as water → copper sulphate solution

---

QUICK TEST

1. If 2 g of solid is dissolved in 100 g of water, what is the mass?

2. What is the solid called?

3. What is the liquid called?

4. If a substance dissolves in a solvent, what is formed?

5. What is a solid which can dissolve called?

6. How does increasing temperature affect how much dissolves?

7. What is a saturated solution?

8. Referring to the graph above, what is the solubility of potassium nitrate at 20°C ?

9. What is the solubility of sodium nitrate at 20°C ?

10. What happens to the solubility of potassium nitrate if it is heated?

10. It becomes more soluble.
9. 900 g per 100 ml of water
8. 400 g per 100 ml of water
7. No more will dissolve at that temperature.
6. Normally the substance becomes more soluble.
5. Soluble
4. A solution
3. The solvent
2. The solute
1. 102 g

CHEMISTRY

DIFFUSION

The movement of particles is called <u>diffusion</u>. Gases <u>diffuse</u> quickly, because the particles are moving <u>very quickly</u> in all directions.

perfume bottle

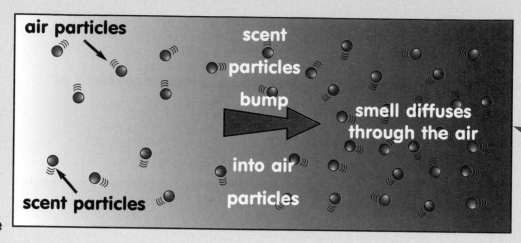

You can <u>smell</u> a perfume because the <u>scent particles diffuse through the air</u> to your nose.

GAS PRESSURE

- Gas particles are moving <u>very quickly</u> in all directions.
- If a gas is put in to a container the gas particles crash into the walls of the container.
- The force of these collisions creates <u>gas pressure</u>.
- If the <u>temperature is increased</u> the gas particles collide <u>harder</u> and <u>more often</u> with the walls of the container, so the pressure <u>increases</u>.
- You can feel the effect of gas pressure when you blow up a balloon.

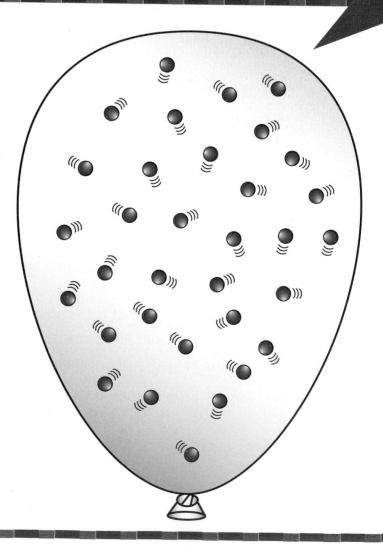

EXPANSION

- When particles are <u>heated</u> they <u>move</u> <u>around</u> more.
- The substance grows <u>bigger</u> (or <u>expands</u>).
- The <u>particles</u> <u>themselves</u> do not get <u>larger</u>, they just take up <u>more</u> <u>space</u> because they are <u>moving more</u>.
- <u>Solids</u>, <u>liquids</u> and <u>gases</u> all expand on heating
- Solids expand the least because the particles are tightly held. Liquids expand more than solids. Gases expand the most of all the states.
- On <u>cooling</u>, substances become <u>smaller</u> (or <u>contract</u>).
- Expansion can exert a lot of <u>force</u>. Concrete roads are constructed with <u>gaps</u> in to allow for expansion in hot weather.

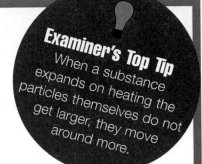

Examiner's Top Tip
When a substance expands on heating the particles themselves do not get larger, they move around more.

PARTICLE THEORY

Particle theory can be used to explain many everyday situations.

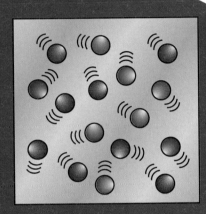

QUICK TEST

1. What is the movement of particles called?
2. Why can you smell a flower across a room?
3. Why do gases diffuse quickly?
4. Can liquids diffuse?
5. What causes pressure?
6. Why does increasing temperature increase the pressure?
7. What happens to the particles as they are heated?
8. Which expands more – a solid or a liquid?
9. Do the particles themselves expand?
10. Why are concrete roads built with gaps in them?

1. Diffusion
2. Scent molecules from the flower diffuse through the air to your nose.
3. Gas particles move quickly in all directions.
4. Yes, but more slowly than gases.
5. When gas particles crash into the walls of a container.
6. Because the gas particles crash into the walls of the container harder and more often.
7. They move around more.
8. A liquid
9. No
10. To allow for expansion in hot weather.

ELEMENTS

- Each element contains only <u>one type of atom</u>.
  There are about <u>100 different elements</u>.
- The <u>periodic table</u> is a helpful way of showing all the elements.
- Each element has a <u>symbol</u> which can be used to <u>identify</u> it.
- For example, <u>carbon</u> can be identified by the symbol <u>C</u>.

Group	I	II										III	IV	V	VI	VII	0/VIII
Period																	
1	H 1																He 2
2	Li 3	Be 4										B 5	C 6	N 7	O 8	F 9	Ne 10
3	Na 11	Mg 12										Al 13	Si 14	P 15	S 16	Cl 17	Ar 18
4	K 19	Ca 20	Sc 21	Ti 22	V 23	Cr 24	Mn 25	Fe 26	Co 27	Ni 28	Cu 29	Zn 30	Ga 31	Ge 32	As 33	Se 34	Br 35	Kr 36
5	Rb 37	Sr 38	Y 39	Zr 40	Nb 41	Mo 42	Tc 43	Ru 44	Rh 45	Pd 46	Ag 47	Cd 48	In 49	Sn 50	Sb 51	Te 52	I 53	Xe 54
6	Cs 55	Ba 56	57 – 71*	Hf 72	Ta 73	W 74	Re 75	Os 76	Ir 77	Pt 78	Au 79	Hg 80	Tl 81	Pb 82	Bi 83	Po 84	At 85	Rn 86
7	Fr 87	Ra 88	89 – 103**	Rf 104	Db 105	Sg 106	Bh 107	Hs 108	Mt 109	Uun 110	Uuu 111	Uub 112	Uut 113	Uuq 114	Uup 115	Uuh 116	Uus 117	Uuo 118

*Lanthanides	La 57	Ce 58	Pr 59	Nd 60	Pm 61	Sm 62	Eu 63	Gd 64	Tb 65	Dy 66	Ho 67	Er 68	Tm 69	Yb 70	Lu 71
**Actinides	Ac 89	Th 90	Pa 91	U 92	Np 93	Pu 94	Am 95	Cm 96	Bk 97	Cf 98	Es 99	Fm 100	Md 101	No 102	Lr 103

Note that elements 113, 115 and 117 are not yet known, but are included in the table to show their respective positions. Elements 114, 116 and 118 have only been reported recently.

Key: ■ Non-metal ■ Metalloid ■ Metal
■ Transitional ■ Rare-earth element (Lanthanide) and radioactive rare-earth element (Actinide)
■ Transactinide □ 'Missing' element

- In the modern periodic table the elements are arranged in order of <u>increasing relative atomic mass</u>.
- The elements are placed in <u>rows</u> so that elements with <u>similar properties</u> are in the same <u>column</u>.
- These vertical columns are called <u>groups</u>.
- The columns are often numbered using <u>roman numerals</u>. For example, Group I consists of Li, Na, K, Rb, Cs, Fr.
- All the members of Group I share similar properties.
- All the elements in <u>Group I</u> have <u>one electron</u> in their <u>outer shell</u>.
- The horizontal rows are called <u>periods</u>.

ATOMS AND ELEMENTS

- Everything is made up of <u>atoms</u>.
- Atoms are extremely <u>small</u>.
- All atoms of the same element have <u>identical</u> numbers of protons.

THE NUCLEUS

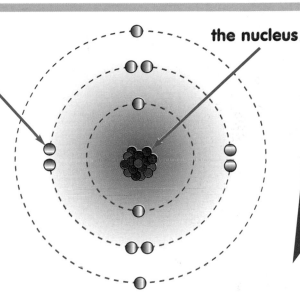

the electrons

the nucleus

- Atoms have a <u>nucleus</u> in the centre, which is surrounded by <u>electrons</u>.
- The nucleus contains <u>neutrons</u> and <u>protons</u>.
- Neutrons have a <u>neutral</u> <u>charge</u> and protons have a <u>positive</u> <u>charge</u>. This means that overall the nucleus has a <u>positive</u> <u>charge</u>.
- The electrons are very, very small, and carry a <u>negative</u> <u>charge</u> as they whiz around the nucleus.

QUICK TEST

1. What is special about an element?
2. How many elements have been discovered?
3. How are the elements often displayed?
4. How are atoms arranged in the periodic table?
5. What are the horizontal rows in the periodic table called?
6. What are the vertical columns in the periodic table called?
7. What is the centre part of an atom called?
8. Which particles are found in the nucleus of an atom?
9. Which particles are found in shells around the nucleus?
10. What charge do electrons have?

10. Negative
9. Electrons
8. Neutrons and protons
7. Nucleus
6. Groups
5. Periods
4. Increasing atomic number
3. Periodic table
2. About 100
1. It only contains one type of atom.

METALS

Three-quarters of the elements in the <u>periodic table</u> are <u>metals</u>.

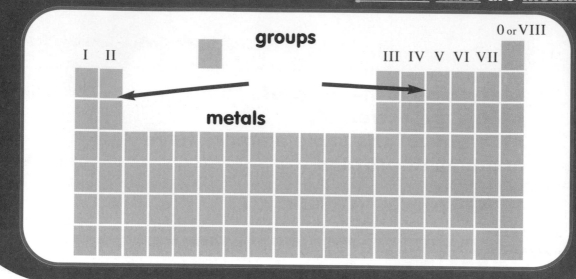

groups

0 or VIII

I II III IV V VI VII

metals

PROPERTIES OF METALS

Metals are good conductors of <u>heat</u>.

Metals have high <u>melting</u> and <u>boiling</u> points. All the metals are solids except mercury which is <u>liquid</u> at room temperature.

Metals are <u>shiny</u> (when freshly cut).

Metals are <u>sonorous</u> (ping when hit).

Metals may be mixed together to form useful <u>alloys</u>.

Metals are good conductors of <u>electricity</u>.

Metals are <u>strong</u> and <u>dense</u>, but they are also <u>malleable</u> (can be hammered into shape) and <u>ductile</u> (can be drawn into wires).

Some metals are <u>magnetic</u> (like iron and steel).

Examiner's Top Tip
Learn the characteristics of metals then cover these pages and write them down. Do the same for non metals.

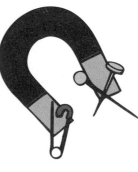

aeroplanes are made of alloys which are light and strong

NON-METALS

- Only 21 elements are non-metals.

non-metals
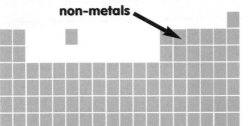

- Non-metals have low melting points and boiling points; 11 of them are gases at room temperature.
- Bromine is the only liquid non-metal at room temperature.

- Non-metals are not <u>shiny</u>, <u>malleable</u>, <u>strong</u>, <u>ductile</u> or <u>sonorous</u>.
- If hit they are <u>brittle</u> and tend to <u>break</u>.
- They appear <u>dull</u>.

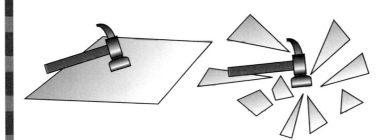

- Non-metals have <u>low</u> <u>densities</u>.

- Non-metals are poor conductors of heat.

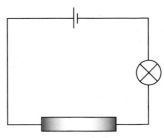

the wooden handle is a poor conductor of heat energy

- Non-metals do not conduct electricity.
- An exception is carbon which, when in the form of graphite, does conduct.

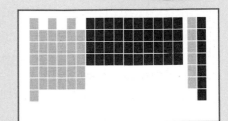

non-metal

electricity cannot flow and the lamp does not light

QUICK TEST

1. Sketch the periodic table and shade the metal elements.
2. Roughly what fraction of the elements are metals?
3. Name the only metal which is not a solid at room temperature.
4. What does sonorous mean ?
5. Name the properties that are common to all metals
6. Roughly what fraction of elements are non-metals?
7. Which non-metal is a liquid at room temperature ?
8. Comment on the density of non-metals.
9. Do non-metals generally conduct electricity ?
10. Which non-metal conducts electricity ?

10. Carbon graphite
9. No
8. Low density
7. bromine
6. $\frac{1}{4}$
5. Good conductors, high m.p. and b.p., strong/dense, malleable and ductile, shiny, sonorous, forms alloys.
4. It pings when hit.
3. Mercury
2. $\frac{3}{4}$
1. see table

UNUSUAL METALS AND NON-METALS

Metals and non-metals have characteristic properties; however, there are certain elements which have unexpected properties.

NON-METALS

Carbon can exist as diamond or graphite.

DIAMOND

- Diamond is a form of the element <u>carbon</u>.
- In diamond all the carbon atoms are held together with <u>very strong bonds</u>.
- Most non-metals are <u>soft</u> or <u>brittle</u>: diamond is very <u>hard</u>.
- Most non-metals are <u>gases</u>, one is a <u>liquid</u> and a few are <u>solids</u> with <u>low melting points</u>.
- Diamond has a very <u>high melting point</u> – over 3500°C.

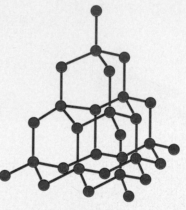

diamond

GRAPHITE

- Graphite is also a form of the element <u>carbon</u>.
- It is made of the same carbon atoms as diamond, but the bonding between the atoms is different. Graphite has a <u>layered structure</u>.
- Most non-metals <u>do not conduct electricity</u>. Graphite is unusual because it can conduct electricity.

electricity may be conducted in this direction

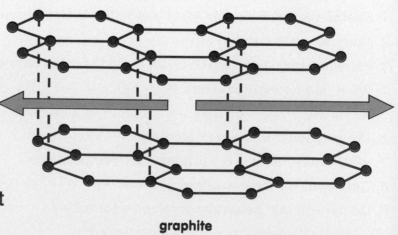

graphite

BROMINE

- Bromine is the only non-metal element which is a <u>liquid</u> at room temperature.

UNUSUAL METALS

MERCURY

Mercury is the only metal which is a <u>liquid</u> at <u>room</u> <u>temperature</u>. All the other metals are <u>solid</u>. Liquids <u>expand</u> more than solids when they are heated, for this reason mercury is used in <u>thermometers</u>.

SODIUM

Sodium is an unusual metal.

- Most metals have a <u>high</u> <u>density</u>: sodium has a much <u>lower</u> <u>density</u> and will even <u>float</u> <u>on</u> <u>water</u>.
- Most metals are <u>hard</u> and <u>strong</u>: sodium is <u>soft</u> and can be cut with a knife.
- Most metals react <u>slowly</u> or <u>not</u> <u>at</u> <u>all</u> with water: sodium reacts <u>very</u> <u>vigorously</u> with water giving off a <u>gas</u> (hydrogen) and forming an <u>alkaline</u> <u>solution</u> (sodium hydroxide).

Examiner's Top Tip
Carbon has two forms: diamond and graphite.

Examiner's Top Tip
Potassium and lithium behave in a similar way to sodium.

QUICK TEST

1. What state are most metals at room temperature?
2. Which is the only metal element which is a liquid at room temperature?
3. What happens to solids and liquids on heating?
4. What is mercury used in?
5. Why does sodium float on water?
6. What happens in the reaction between sodium and water?
7. Name two forms of carbon.
8. Why is diamond unusual for a non-metal?
9. Why is graphite unusual for a non-metal?
10. Which is the only non-metal which is liquid at room temperature?

1. Solid 2. Mercury 3. They expand 4. Thermometers 5. It is less dense than water. 6. It is very vigorous and hydrogen and sodium hydroxide are produced. 7. Diamond and graphite 8. It is hard and has a very high melting point. 9. It conducts electricity. 10. Bromine

THE RUSTING OF IRON

The rusting of <u>iron</u> <u>and</u> <u>steel</u> is an important <u>everyday</u> <u>chemical</u> <u>reaction</u>.
It is not a useful reaction, and we try to <u>slow</u> <u>down</u> or <u>stop</u> the reaction.

CORRODING OF IRON

Iron corrodes (or rusts) faster than most metals.
Three test tubes are set up in an experiment and left for a few days.

Examiner's Top Tip
The rusting of iron has a very slow rate of reaction.

nail in air + water
rust on nail

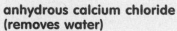
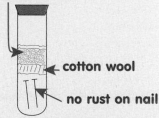

anhydrous calcium chloride (removes water)
cotton wool
no rust on nail

oil (prevents air getting in)
boiled water (no oxygen)
no rust on nail

TEST TUBE 1

<u>Air</u> (which contains oxygen) and <u>water</u> are both present.
air and water are present

TEST TUBE 2

Air is present but there is no water. <u>Anhydrous</u> <u>calcium</u> <u>chloride</u> removes any water from the air.
air is present

TEST TUBE 3

The nails are resting in <u>water</u>. Although there is air in the test tube, any air <u>dissolved</u> in the water has been removed by boiling it. A <u>layer</u> <u>of</u> <u>oil</u> on top of the water stops any air from reaching the water.
water is present

After a few days <u>rusting</u> has only occurred in test tube 1.
Both <u>oxygen</u> <u>and</u> <u>water</u> <u>must</u> <u>be</u> <u>present</u> for rusting to happen.
If either the oxygen or the water is <u>completely</u> <u>removed</u> then the iron will not rust.

Examiner's Top Tip
Water and oxygen must both be present for rusting to occur.

PREVENTING RUSTING

COATING THE IRON OR STEEL

- *Painting* the iron or *coating* the iron in plastic or oil can stop oxygen and water from reaching the iron, but if the coating is *damaged* the iron will *rust*.
- Steel *cars* are painted to stop them from rusting, but if this *protective layer* is damaged then the air and water can reach the steel, and it will rust.

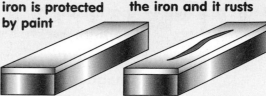

iron is protected by paint

if the layer is scratched water and air reaches the iron and it rusts

no rusting occurs

if it is scratched rusting occurs

TIN PLATING

- If the iron is plated with *tin* or *chromium* it will not rust. Tin and chromium are both *less reactive* than iron. However, if the protective layer is damaged then it will begin to rust.

surgical instruments can be made from stainless steel

ALLOYING THE METAL

- If the iron is mixed with other metals such as chromium it will form the alloy *stainless steel*.
- This does not rust.

speed boat engines are protected using zinc or magnesium

SACRIFICIAL PROTECTION

- If a metal which is more reactive than iron, such as *zinc* or *magnesium*, is connected to the iron corrosion will be prevented. Because the zinc is more reactive, the zinc reacts instead of the iron.
- The iron is protected at the expense of the more reactive metal. For this reason it is called *sacrificial protection*.

QUICK TEST

1. What does anhydrous calcium chloride do?
2. Why is the water boiled in test tube 3 of the experiment described on page 62?
3. Why is a layer of oil placed on top of the water in test tube 3?
4. How can painting steel cars prevent them from rusting?
5. What would happen if the paint was scratched?
6. What two things are needed for iron to rust?
7. What can be used to coat iron and prevent rusting?
8. How is stainless steel made and what are its advantages?
9. What is sacrificial protection?
10. Give an example of sacrificial protection.

1. It removes water
2. It removes air dissolved in water.
3. To stop air reaching the water.
4. It stops air and water reaching the metal.
5. The metal would rust.
6. Oxygen and water
7. Paint/plastic/oil
8. By alloying iron with Chromium (Cr), that does not rust.
9. When magnesium (Mg) or zinc (Zn) is in contact with iron (Fe), Fe is protected as Mg/Zn reacts first.
10. It is used to protect boat engines, etc

REACTIVITY SERIES

Most reactive —	potassium K sodium Na calcium Ca magnesium Mg **carbon C**	**Extracted from their ores by <u>electrolysis</u>**
	zinc Zn iron Fe lead Pb <u>hydrogen</u> **H**	**Extracted from their ores by heating with <u>carbon</u> (coke or charcoal)**
Least reactive —	copper Cu gold Au	**Metals less reactive than hydrogen <u>do</u> <u>not</u> react with water or dilute acids**

This order has been worked out by observing how vigorous the <u>reaction</u> is between the metal and:

- **air;**
- **water; and**
- **dilute acid.**

REACTIVITY SERIES

**Some metals are more reactive than others.
The metals can be placed in order of reactivity.**

When metals are heated with air they may react with the oxygen present.

metal + oxygen ⟹ *metal oxide*

magnesium + oxygen ⟹ *magnesium oxide*

$2Mg(s) + O_2(g)$ ⟹ $2MgO(s)$

Most reactive –	potassium K sodium Na calcium Ca magnesium Mg	**These metals react vigorously. They <u>burn</u> fiercely.**
	<u>carbon C</u> zinc Zn iron Fe lead Pb <u>hydrogen H</u> copper Cu	**These metals react <u>slowly</u> with air.**
Least reactive –	gold Au	**No reaction**

REACTING METALS WITH WATER

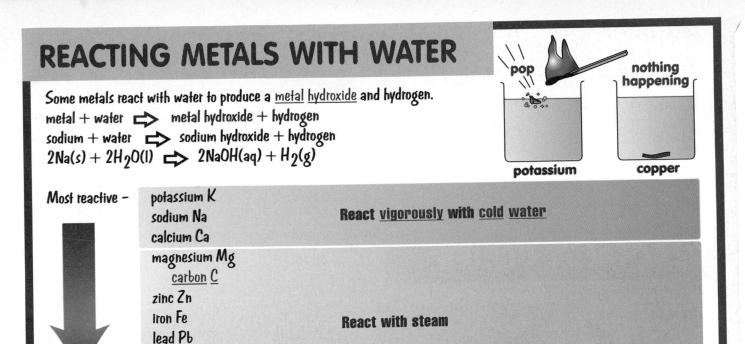

Some metals react with water to produce a <u>metal hydroxide</u> and hydrogen.

metal + water ⇨ metal hydroxide + hydrogen

sodium + water ⇨ sodium hydroxide + hydrogen

$2Na(s) + 2H_2O(l) \Rightarrow 2NaOH(aq) + H_2(g)$

Most reactive –

potassium K sodium Na calcium Ca	React <u>vigorously</u> with <u>cold</u> <u>water</u>
magnesium Mg <u>carbon C</u> zinc Zn iron Fe lead Pb <u>hydrogen H</u>	React with steam
copper Cu gold Au	No reaction

Least reactive –

REACTING METALS WITH DILUTE ACIDS

Some metals (those more reactive than hydrogen) react with <u>dilute</u> <u>acids</u> to produce salts and hydrogen.

metal + acid ⇨ salt + hydrogen

calcium + hydrochloric acid ⇨ calcium chloride + hydrogen

$Ca(s) + 2HCl(aq) \Rightarrow CaCl_2(aq) + H_2(g)$

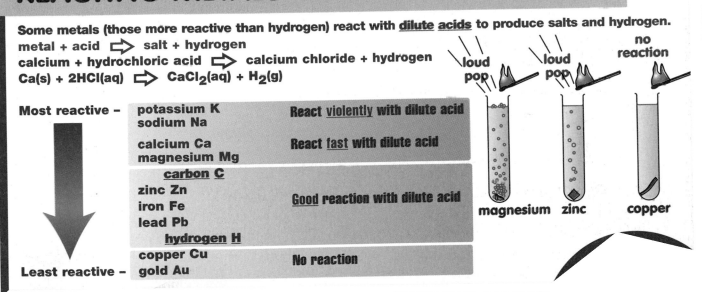

Most reactive –

potassium K sodium Na	React <u>violently</u> with dilute acid
calcium Ca magnesium Mg	React <u>fast</u> with dilute acid
<u>carbon C</u> zinc Zn iron Fe lead Pb <u>hydrogen H</u>	<u>Good</u> reaction with dilute acid
copper Cu gold Au	No reaction

Least reactive –

QUICK TEST

1. How should metals more reactive than carbon be extracted from their ores?
2. How should metals less reactive than carbon be extracted from their ores?
3. How was the reactivity series compiled?
4. When metals burn in oxygen what is formed?
5. What is formed when zinc is burnt in air?
6. Give a balanced equation for the reaction.
7. What is formed when potassium reacts with water?
8. Give a balanced equation for the reaction.
9. What forms when magnesium reacts with hydrochloric acid?
10. Give a balanced equation for the reaction.

METAL DISPLACEMENT REACTIONS

A more reactive metal will displace a less reactive metal from a compound.

Most reactive	potassium K
	sodium Na
	calcium Ca
	magnesium Mg
	carbon C
	zinc Zn
	iron Fe
	lead Pb
	hydrogen H
	copper Cu
Least reactive	gold Au

IRON AND COPPER SULPHATE
Iron is more reactive than copper.
- When an iron nail is placed in a solution of copper sulphate, the nail changes colour from silver to orange–pink.
- The nail has been coated with copper.
- The solution changes colour from blue to a very pale green.
- The solution now contains iron sulphate.

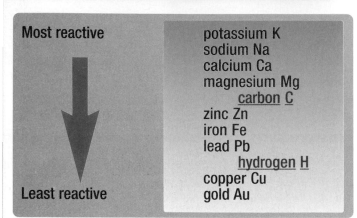

what you observe

This is an example of a displacement reaction. The more reactive metal, iron, displaces the less reactive metal, copper, from its compound, copper sulphate.

iron + copper sulphate $\Rightarrow$ copper + iron sulphate
iron is more reactive
$Fe(s) + CuSO_4(aq) \Rightarrow Cu(s) + FeSO_4(aq)$
copper is less reactive

iron displaces the copper from the solution
the copper is displaced

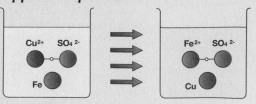

what the ions are doing

ZINC AND IRON SULPHATE
- Using the reactivity series, zinc is more reactive than iron.
- The zinc displaces the iron from the solution.

zinc + iron sulphate $\Rightarrow$ zinc sulphate + iron
$Zn(s) + FeSO_4(aq) \Rightarrow ZnSO_4(aq) + Fe(s)$

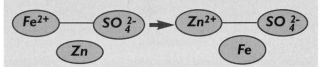

- This shows that zinc is more reactive than iron and iron is more reactive than copper.

The order of reactivity is:

most   zinc

        iron

least   copper

Examiner's Top Tip
An understanding of the reactivity series and displacement reactions can help you to predict and explain many chemical reactions.

COPPER AND MAGNESIUM SULPHATE
If the metal which is added is less reactive than the metal in the compound then no reaction will occur.

copper + magnesium sulphate $\Rightarrow$ no rea[...]

THE THERMIT REACTION

This is a very useful <u>displacement</u> <u>reaction</u>.

It is used to produce <u>molten</u> <u>iron</u> to mend railway tracks.

- Aluminium is heated with iron oxide.
- Aluminium is more reactive than iron, so the aluminium <u>displaces</u> the iron.
- Aluminium oxide and iron are produced.

The reaction gives out a lot of heat, or is very <u>exothermic</u>; the iron produced is molten and can therefore be poured into gaps in the rails.

Aluminium + iron oxide $\Rightarrow$ aluminium oxide + iron

Examiner's Top Tip
Exothermic reactions give out heat energy.

QUICK TEST

1. What is the rule for displacement reactions ?
2. Which metal is more reactive: iron or copper ?
3. What is the word equation for the reaction between iron and copper sulphate?
4. Write a balanced symbol equation for the reaction?
5. Which metal is the more reactive: iron or zinc ?
6. What is the word equation for the reaction between zinc and iron sulphate?
7. Write a balanced symbol equation for the reaction?
8. Which metal is more reactive: copper or magnesium?
9. Write a word equation for the reaction between magnesium and copper sulphate.
10. What happens when copper is placed in a solution of zinc sulphate ?

1. A more reactive metal will displace a less reactive metal from a compound.
2. Iron
3. iron + copper sulphate $\Rightarrow$ iron sulphate + copper
4. Fe(s) + CuSO$_4$(aq) $\Rightarrow$ FeSO$_4$(aq) + Cu(s)
5. Zinc
6. zinc + iron sulphate $\Rightarrow$ zinc sulphate + iron
7. Zn(s) + FeSO$_4$(aq) $\Rightarrow$ ZnSO$_4$(aq) + Fe(s)
8. Magnesium
9. magnesium + copper sulphate $\Rightarrow$ magnesium sulphate + copper
10. No reaction.

INDICATORS

• There are many different indicators.

Indicator	Acid	Neutral	Alkali
Universal Indicator	red	green	purple
Blue litmus	red	blue	blue
Red litmus	red	red	blue
Phenolphthalein	colourless	colourless	pink

1 2 3 4 5 6 7 8 9 10 11 12 13 14

← ACIDS   ALKALIS →

ACIDS

Acidic solutions have a pH less than 7.
The strongest acids have a pH of 1.
The weakest acids have a pH of 6.

COMMON ACIDS ARE:
• hydrochloric acid
• sulphuric acid
• nitric acid

The soluble oxides of non-metals form acidic solutions.

ALKALIS

Alkalis are also called bases.
Alkalis are soluble bases.
Alkalis have a pH of more than 7.
The strongest alkalis have a pH of 14.
The weakest alkalis have a pH of 8.

COMMON ALKALIS ARE:
• sodium hydroxide
• potassium hydroxide
• calcium hydroxide

TREATING SOILS

• Many plants only grow really well at a certain pH.
• Food crops in particular do not thrive if the soil is too acidic.
• Farmers add lime to the soil to neutralise the acid so the pH of the soil is right for the plant that is being grown.

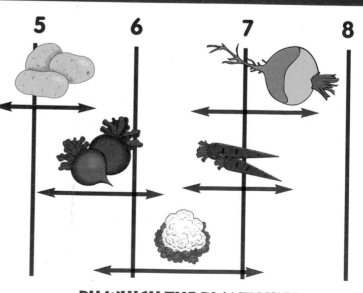

5   6   7   8

PH WHICH THE PLANT LIKES

ACIDS AND ALKALIS

Indicators are used to show whether a solution is acidic, alkaline or neutral by changing colour.

TREATING INDIGESTION

Examiner's Top Tip
Hydrogen, H^+ ions make solutions acidic.

- Your stomach contains <u>hydrochloric acid</u>.
- It helps you to digest your food.
- If more acid than usual is produced you get <u>indigestion</u>.
- To stop this indigestion this <u>extra acid</u> needs to be neutralised with an alkali.

- Some indigestion tablets contain calcium carbonate.

hydrochloric acid + calcium carbonate ⇨ calcium chloride + water + carbon dioxide

| extra acid in the stomach | base in the indigestion tablet | salt | water |

Examiner's Top Tip
Learn what colour indicators will be in different types of solution.

NEUTRALISATION

The reaction between an acid and a base is called <u>neutralisation</u>.
acid + alkali ⇨ a neutral salt + water

The type of salt produced depends on the metal in the alkali used and on the acid used.

Examiner's Top Tip
Learn these uses of neutralisation.

QUICK TEST

1. What colour is Universal Indicator in neutral solution?

2. What colour is blue litmus in neutral solution?

3. What colour is blue litmus in an acid?

4. What is the pH of a neutral solution?

5. What is the pH of the strongest alkali?

6. What is the pH of a weak acid?

7. What colour is Universal Indicator in water?

8. What colour is red litmus in water?

9. How are alkalis and bases related?

10. Name three common acids.

10. Hydrochloric acid, sulphuric acid, nitric acid.
9. Alkalis are soluble bases.
8. Red
7. Green
6. 6
5. 14
4. 7
3. Red
2. Blue
1. Green

METAL CARBONATES

Metal carbonates can be <u>neutralised</u> by acids.

Most carbonates are <u>insoluble</u>, so they are bases, but they are not alkalis.

When carbonates are neutralised carbon dioxide is given off:

<u>metal</u> <u>carbonate</u> + <u>acid</u> ⟹ <u>salt</u> + <u>water</u> + <u>carbon dioxide</u>

copper carbonate + hydrochloric acid ⟹ copper chloride + water + carbon dioxide

$CuCO_3(s)$ + $2HCl(aq)$ ⟹ $CuCl_2(aq)$ + $H_2O(l)$ + $CO_2(g)$

zinc carbonate + sulphuric acid ⟹ zinc sulphate + water + carbon dioxide

$ZnCO_3(s)$ + $H_2SO_4(aq)$ ⟹ $ZnSO_4(aq)$ + $H_2O(l)$ + $CO_2(g)$

MAKING COPPER CHLORIDE

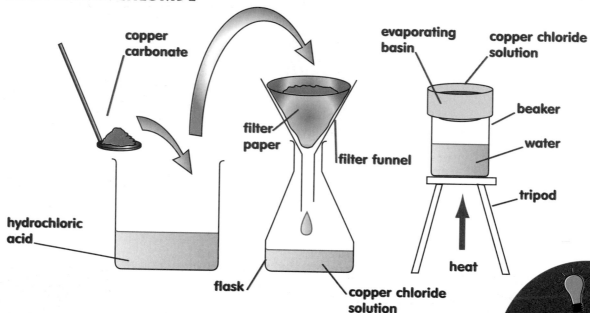

- Copper carbonate is added to the acid until it stops fizzing.
- The unreacted copper carbonate is then removed by <u>filtering</u>.
- The solution is poured into an evaporating dish.
- It is heated until the first crystals appear.
- The solution is then left for a few days for the copper chloride to <u>crystallise</u>.

Examiner's Top Tip
Sulphuric acid makes sulphate salts. Hydrochloric acid makes chloride salts. Nitric acid makes nitrate salts.

METALS

Metals can be reacted with acids to form a salt and hydrogen:

- <u>metal</u> + <u>acid</u> ⟹ <u>salt</u> + <u>hydrogen</u>

zinc + hydrochloric acid ⟹ zinc chloride + hydrogen

$Zn(s) + 2HCl(aq)$ ⟹ $ZnCl_2(aq)$ + $H_2(g)$

magnesium + sulphuric acid ⟹ magnesium sulphate + hydrogen

$Mg(s)$ + $H_2SO_4(aq)$ ⟹ $MgSO_4(aq)$ + $H_2(g)$

METAL OXIDES

Metal oxides are also bases; they can be reacted with acids to make salts and water:

- metal oxide + acid $\Rightarrow$ salt + water

copper oxide + hydrochloric acid $\Rightarrow$ copper chloride + water

$CuO(s)$ + $2HCl(aq)$ $\Rightarrow$ $CuCl_2(aq)$ + $H_2O(l)$

zinc oxide + sulphuric acid $\Rightarrow$ zinc sulphate + water

$ZnO(s)$ + $H_2SO_4(aq)$ $\Rightarrow$ $ZnSO_4(aq)$ + $H_2O(l)$

MAKING SALTS

METAL HYDROXIDES

We have seen that metal hydroxides can be neutralised with acids to make salt and water:

metal hydroxide + acid $\Rightarrow$ salt + water

QUICK TEST

1. What is formed when hydrochloric acid reacts with potassium hydroxide?
2. What is formed when sulphuric acid reacts with sodium hydroxide?
3. Which gas is given off when carbonates react with acid?
4. What is formed when hydrochloric acid reacts with zinc carbonate?
5. What is formed when sulphuric acid reacts with magnesium carbonate?
6. How could you get a sample of a soluble salt?
7. What is formed when hydrochloric acid reacts with magnesium?
8. What is formed when sulphuric acid reacts with zinc?
9. What is formed when hydrochloric acid reacts with zinc oxide?
10. What is formed when sulphuric acid reacts with copper oxide?

1. Potassium chloride + water
2. Sodium sulphate + water
3. Carbon dioxide
4. Zinc chloride + water + carbon dioxide
5. Magnesium sulphate + water + carbon dioxide
6. Remove unreacted solid by filtering, then evaporate off the water
7. Magnesium chloride + hydrogen
8. Zinc sulphate + hydrogen
9. Zinc chloride + water
10. Copper sulphate + water

COMMON TESTS AND APPARATUS

COMMON TESTS

CARBON DIOXIDE
The gas is <u>bubbled</u> through <u>limewater</u>.
Carbon dioxide turns limewater <u>milky</u>.

HYDROGEN
If a lighted splint is nearby hydrogen will burn with a '<u>squeaky pop</u>'.

OXYGEN
Oxygen <u>relights</u> a glowing <u>splint</u>.

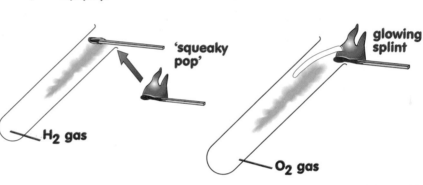

CO_2 gas

limewater

'squeaky pop'

H_2 gas

glowing splint

O_2 gas

Examiner's Top Tip
Choose apparatus which is suitable for the job.

APPARATUS

Below is some of the apparatus found in the science laboratory.

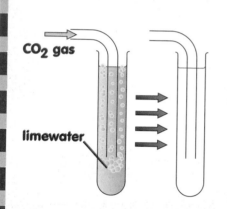

conical flask

measuring cylinder

triangle

beaker

evaporating basin

spatula

tripod

Bunsen burner

filter funnel

test tube

boss
clamp
stand

gauze

thermometer

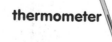

Examiner's Top Tip
Some chemicals carry more than one hazard.

SAFETY HAZARDS

OXIDISING
- Provides <u>oxygen</u> which allows <u>other</u> <u>materials</u> to burn <u>more</u> <u>fiercely</u>.

HARMFUL
- Similar to <u>toxic</u> but less dangerous.

HIGHLY FLAMMABLE
- Catches fire easily.

CORROSIVE
- Attacks and destroys <u>living tissues</u>, including <u>eyes</u> and <u>skin</u>.

TOXIC
- Can cause <u>death</u>, if <u>swallowed</u>, <u>breathed</u> in or <u>absorbed</u> through the skin.

IRRITANT
- Not corrosive but can cause reddening or blistering of the skin.

QUICK TEST

1. Sketch the hazard symbol for oxidising.
2. Sketch the hazard symbol for highly flammable.
3. Sketch the hazard symbol for toxic.
4. Sketch the hazard symbol for corrosive.
5. Sketch the hazard symbol for irritant.
6. Sketch the hazard symbol for harmful.
7. What is the test for carbon dioxide?
8. What is the test for hydrogen?
9. Which piece of apparatus would you use to measure the volume of a liquid?
10. Which piece of apparatus would you use to separate a solid from a liquid?

Examiner's Top Tip
None of this is hard, it is just a case of learning all the points.

10. Filter funnel.
9. A measuring cylinder.
8. Lighted splint gives 'squeaky pop'.
7. Gas is bubbled through limewater which turns milky.
6. See above
5. See above
4. See above
3. See above
2. See above
1. See above

73

MIXTURES

If there are <u>two</u> <u>or</u> <u>more</u> different <u>atoms</u>, but they are <u>not</u> <u>joined</u>, they are a <u>mixture</u> of different <u>elements</u>.

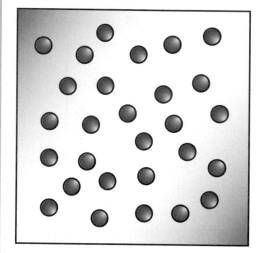

If there are two or more different <u>compounds</u>, but they are <u>not</u> joined, they are a mixture of <u>compounds</u>.

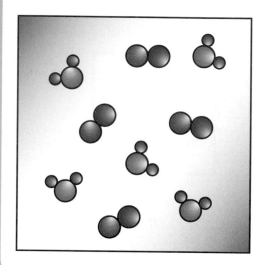

FIXED COMPOSITION

- A mixture contains <u>two or more</u> atoms or compounds that are not combined or joined together.
- Mixtures are <u>easy to separate</u>.
- Compounds are much <u>harder to separate</u>.
- Mixtures <u>do not</u> have a <u>fixed composition</u>.
- Compounds <u>do</u> have a fixed composition.

SEA WATER

Sea water is a <u>mixture</u>. It contains particles of water, salts and gases. These particles are mixed together, but they are not joined.

AIR

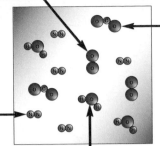

a molecule of oxygen, an element

a molecule of carbon dioxide, a compound consisting of carbon and oxygen

a molecule of nitrogen, an element

a molecule of water, a compound consisting of oxygen and hydrogen

Air is a mixture of <u>gas</u> particles. Air is composed of about <u>80%</u> <u>nitrogen</u> molecules and about <u>20%</u> <u>oxygen</u> molecules. There are also very small amounts of other gases, including <u>carbon dioxide</u>, <u>water vapour</u> and <u>Noble gases</u>, including <u>argon</u> and <u>neon</u>. These gas particles are <u>mixed</u> together, but they are not <u>joined</u>.

ROCKS

- Most rocks contain a mixture of different minerals.
- Minerals are compounds because they have a fixed composition.
- Granite is an <u>igneous</u> rock.
- It contains a mixture of minerals.
- It consists mainly of the minerals <u>feldspar</u>, <u>quartz</u> and <u>mica</u>.
- The exact proportion of these minerals is not <u>fixed</u>, and will vary from rock to rock.

QUICK TEST

1. Can mixtures be separated easily?
2. Why is a mixture different to a compound?
3. Can you have a mixture of compounds?
4. Do compounds have a fixed composition?
5. Do mixtures have a fixed composition?
6. Is sea water a mixture?
7. What does sea water contain?
8. What does air contain?
9. What percentage of air is nitrogen?
10. What are most rocks a mixture of?

Examiner's Top Tip
Learn the examples of mixtures discussed on this spread.

10. Different minerals
9. 80%
8. Nitrogen, oxygen, water vapour, carbon dioxide, argon and neon
7. Water, salts and gases
6. Yes
5. No
4. Yes
3. Yes
2. It is not joined
1. Yes

SEPARATION TECHNIQUES

- In a mixture the constituent parts are **not joined together**.
- Mixtures can be **separated** quite easily.

FILTRATION

- *Filtration is used to **separate** a mixture of a solid and a liquid.*
- *The mixture is poured through a **filter paper**. Only the liquid passes through and is called the **filtrate**. The solid is collected on the filter paper and is called the **residue**.*

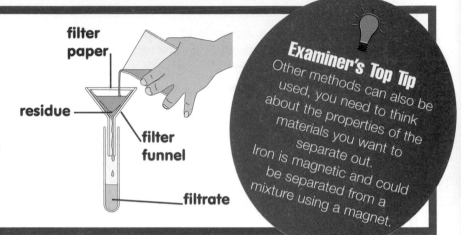

filter paper

residue

filter funnel

filtrate

FILTRATION AND EVAPORATION

- A mixture of <u>salt</u> and <u>sand</u> can be <u>separated</u> using these two techniques.
  When water is added and the mixture is stirred, the <u>soluble</u> <u>salt</u> will <u>dissolve</u>.
  The <u>insoluble</u> <u>sand</u> does not dissolve.
  The mixture can then be <u>filtered</u>: the <u>dissolved</u> <u>salt</u> passes through the filter, while the sand can be <u>collected</u> from the filter paper.

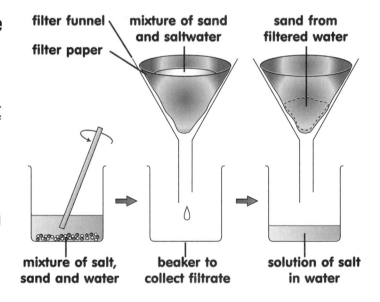

filter funnel

filter paper

mixture of sand and saltwater

sand from filtered water

mixture of salt, sand and water

beaker to collect filtrate

solution of salt in water

- Solutions of a <u>solvent</u> and a <u>solute</u> can be separated by <u>evaporation</u>.
  The <u>solvent</u>, in this case water, can be evaporated, leaving the solute (salt) behind.
  The salt forms <u>crystals</u>; this process is called <u>crystallisation</u>.

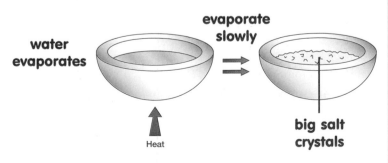

water evaporates

evaporate slowly

Heat

big salt crystals

CHROMATOGRAPHY

- Chromatography can be used to separate mixtures of different coloured dyes. The different dyes have different solubilities.
- This method can be used to find which dyes make up black ink.
  A spot of ink is placed on a piece of filter paper and this is placed in a beaker containing a small amount of solvent.
  The solvent travels across the filter paper carrying the dyes with it.
  Each dye has a slightly different solubility, so travels a slightly different distance across the paper.
- This black dye contains red, blue and yellow dyes.

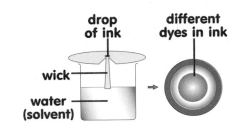

drop of ink   different dyes in ink
wick
water (solvent)

DISTILLATION

DISTILLATION

- Distillation can be used to separate a solvent from a solution.
- It can be used to separate water from a solution of salt and water. The solution is heated. The water boils and water vapour is formed. The water vapour cools and condenses to form liquid water which is collected in a beaker. This water is called 'distilled water' and is very pure.

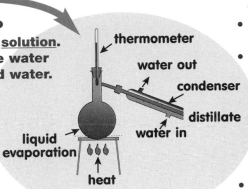

thermometer
water out
condenser
distillate
water in
liquid evaporation
heat

FRACTIONAL DISTILLATION

- Fractional distillation can be used to separate a mixture of two or more liquids.
- It can be used to separate alcohol and water.
- The liquids still boil at their own boiling temperatures, even though they are now in a mixture. The alcohol boils at 78°C. Some water will also evaporate, but it will condense in the fractionating column and fall back into the flask.
- Only the alcohol passes into the condenser, where it forms pure liquid alcohol which is collected in the beaker.

QUICK TEST

1. In a mixture are the constituent parts joined?

2. In a compound are the constituent parts joined?

3. How should a mixture of solid and liquid be separated?

4. How can crystals of a salt be obtained from a mixture of salt and water?

5. Which technique should be used to separate a mixture of different coloured dyes?

6. Why do different dyes travel different distances?

7. How can water be separated from a mixture of salt and water?

8. What is the name of the piece of equipment in which the water vapour is turned back into liquid water?

9. How can a mixture of alcohol and water be separated?

10. In a mixture of alcohol and water, which boils first?

FORMING COMPOUNDS

- During a chemical reaction a <u>new</u> <u>substance</u> is made.
- These new chemicals are the <u>products</u> of the reaction. The starting chemicals are called the <u>reactants</u>.
- The products can have <u>very</u> <u>different</u> <u>properties</u> from the reactants.

  Heating iron with sulphur gives iron sulphide.

Iron	+	sulphur	$\longrightarrow$	iron sulphide
Fe	+	S	$\longrightarrow$	FeS

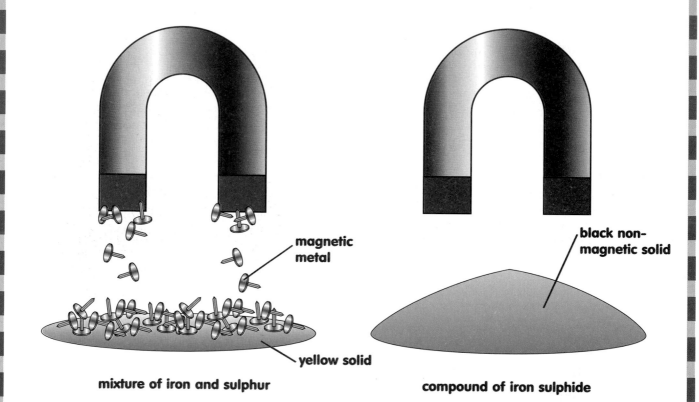

magnetic metal

yellow solid

mixture of iron and sulphur

black non-magnetic solid

compound of iron sulphide

- A compound has a fixed composition. Iron sulphide FeS
- contains one atom of iron and one atom of sulphur joined together.

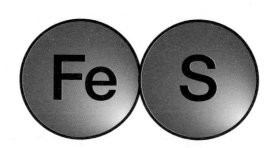

COMPOUNDS

Atoms may form molecules. A molecule is where two or more atoms are joined together.

- If the atoms are of the same element, they form a <u>molecule</u> of the <u>element</u>.

- If atoms of two or more elements are joined together, they form <u>molecules</u> of a <u>compound</u>.

QUICK TEST

1. What does this represent?

2. What does this represent?

3. What does this represent?

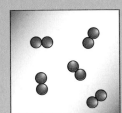

Examiner's Top Tip
Things to look out for to show a chemical reaction is happening:
- bubbles – these show a gas is being made
- a change in colour
- a change in temperature – usually an increase as most reactions are exothermic.

4. If you saw bubbles during a chemical reaction, what is being made?

5. What piece of apparatus would you use to find if the temperature had increased?

6. What are the chemicals at the start of a chemical reaction called?

7. What are the chemicals made by a chemical reaction called?

8. How can you tell if a chemical reaction has occurred when iron and sulphur are heated to form iron sulphide?

9. Do compounds have a fixed composition?

10. Can the elements in a compound be separated easily?

10. No.
9. Yes
8. Iron is no longer magnetic, there is change in colour, etc
7. Products
6. Reactants
5. Thermometer
4. Gas
3. Molecules of a compound
2. Molecules of an element
1. Atoms of two elements

CHANGING THE NAMES

If atoms of two elements join together in a chemical reaction, it can be represented in a <u>word equation</u>:

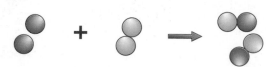

sodium   chlorine

sodium chloride (a compound)

-    sodium   +   chlorine   ⇨   sodium chloride

This can also be represented using <u>symbols</u>:

-    2Na   + Cl_2 ⇨   2NaCl

The name of the compound is given by the two elements that have joined.

- The <u>chlorine</u> has changed to <u>chloride</u>.

In a similar way the names of these non-metals change when they form compounds.

- oxygen ⇨ oxide
- fluorine ⇨ fluoride
- bromine ⇨ bromide
- iodine ⇨ iodide
- sulphur ⇨ sulphide

magnesium   oxygen

magnesium oxide (a compound)

Therefore,

   magnesium   +   oxygen   ⇨   magnesium oxide

or

   2Mg   + O_2 ⇨   2MgO

Examiner's Top Tip
In all chemical reactions the overall mass does not change. Overall mass before = overall mass after the reaction.

CARBON DIOXIDE (CO_2)

Carbon dioxide is formed from <u>one carbon</u> and <u>two oxygen</u> atoms.

- carbon + oxygen ⇨ carbon dioxide

The <u>di</u> shows that there are <u>two</u> oxygen atoms.

carbon   oxygen

carbon dioxide (a compound)

NAMING COMPOUNDS

When atoms of two or more elements join together they form a <u>compound</u>. Compounds are <u>difficult</u> <u>to</u> <u>separate</u>.

WATER (H₂O)

Water is formed from <u>two</u> <u>hydrogen</u> atoms and <u>one</u> <u>oxygen</u> atom.

• hydrogen + oxygen ⇨ water

hydrogen   oxygen   water (a compound)

Examiner's Top Tip
Compounds have a fixed composition.

QUICK TEST

1. Can components in a mixture be separated easily?

2. Can elements in a compound be separated easily?

3. What is a compound?

4. What is the name of the compound formed when magnesium reacts with oxygen?

5. What is the name of the compound formed when magnesium reacts with bromine?

6. In the compound magnesium chloride, MgCl₂ how many atoms of magnesium and chlorine are present?

7. In the compound carbon <u>monoxide</u> CO, how many atoms of carbon and oxygen are present?

8. Write a word equation for the reaction between sodium and chlorine.

9. Write a word equation for the reaction between hydrogen and oxygen.

10. Write a word equation for the reaction between magnesium and oxygen.

1. Yes
2. No
3. When atoms of two or more elements are joined together.
4. Magnesium oxide
5. Magnesium bromide
6. 1 Mg and 2 Cl
7. 1 C and 1 O
8. sodium + chlorine ⇨ sodium chloride
9. hydrogen + oxygen ⇨ water
10. magnesium + oxygen ⇨ magnesium oxide

BALANCING THE EQUATION

When <u>hydrogen</u> burns in <u>oxygen</u>, <u>water</u> is made.

- <u>Hydrogen</u> + <u>oxygen</u> ⇨ <u>water</u>

- H_2 + O_2 ⇨ H_2O

The <u>formulae</u> are correct, but the equation is <u>not</u> balanced because there are different numbers of atoms on each side of the equation. The formulae <u>cannot</u> be changed, but the numbers in front of the formulae <u>can</u> be changed.

HOW TO BALANCE AN EQUATION

Looking at the equation we can see that there are <u>two</u> oxygen atoms on the left-hand side but only <u>one</u> on the right-hand side.

So a <u>2</u> is placed <u>in front</u> of the H_2O:

- H_2 + O_2 ⇨ $2H_2O$

Now the oxygen atoms are balanced, but while there are <u>two</u> hydrogen atoms on the left-hand side there are <u>four</u> hydrogen atoms on the right-hand side.

So a <u>2</u> is placed in front of the H_2:

- $2H_2$ + O_2 ⇨ $2H_2O$

- **The equation is then balanced.**

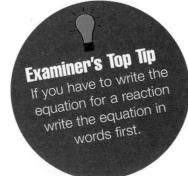

Examiner's Top Tip
If you have to write the equation for a reaction write the equation in words first.

CHEMICAL FORMULAE

- Symbol equations show the number of atoms.
- The chemical formula for water is H_2O.
- This means that every water molecule consists of two hydrogen atoms and one oxygen atom.

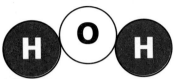

- The chemical formula for copper sulphate is $CuSO_4$.
- This means that every copper sulphate molecule consists of one copper atom, one sulphur atom and four oxygen atoms.
- When a chemical reaction takes place it can be represented using a <u>balanced</u> equation.
- There must be the same number of atoms on <u>both</u> <u>sides</u> of the equation. Atoms <u>cannot</u> <u>be</u> <u>created</u> <u>or</u> <u>destroyed</u>.
- This means that in chemical changes the overall mass before and after is the same.

Examiner's Top Tip
Balancing equations just needs a little practise – deal with the atoms one at a time until everything balances.

BALANCING EQUATIONS

QUICK TEST

Examiner's Top Tip
When balancing an equation always check that the formulae you have written down are correct.

Consider $CaCO_3$

1. How many calcium atoms are present?

2. How many carbon atoms are present?

3. How many oxygen atoms are present?

Consider H_2SO_4

4. How many hydrogen atoms are present?

5. How many sulphur atoms are present?

6. How many oxygen atoms are present?

7. Why must there be the same number of atoms on both sides of the equation?

8. Balance the equation $Na(s) + Cl_2(g) \Rightarrow NaCl(s)$

9. Balance the equation $H_2(g) + Cl_2(g) \Rightarrow HCl(g)$

10. Balance the equation $C(s) + CO_2(g) \Rightarrow CO(g)$

10. $C(s) + CO_2(g) \Rightarrow 2CO(g)$
9. $H_2(g) + Cl_2(g) \Rightarrow 2HCl(g)$
8. $2 Na(s) + Cl_2(g) \Rightarrow 2NaCl(s)$
7. Atoms cannot be created or destroyed.
6. Four
5. One
4. Two
3. Three
2. One
1. One

EXAM QUESTIONS –

1. The table shows the pH of four solutions.
   Which of the solutions is
   a) an acid
   b) a neutral solution
   c) an alkali?

Solution	pH of solution
A	10
B	6
C	2
D	7

2. Melting and condensing are the names of two changes of state. Explain the changes these terms represent.
   a) melting...
   b) condensing...

3. The diagram shows a cross section of rock.
   Which rock is probably the oldest?

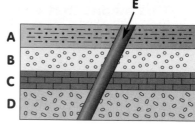

a cross section of rock

4. A magnet was used to find out which objects were magnetic.
   Complete the results:

   Object tested   Attracted to magnet
   plastic knife   ....
   steel pin   ....
   iron nail   ....
   wooden ruler   ....
   aluminium foil   ....

5. a) Fill in the missing word:
   When a solid is dissolved in a solvent it forms a ....
   b) A beaker containing water is placed on a balance. It has a mass of 100.0 g.
      5.5 g of salt is dissolved in the water. It can no longer be seen.
   What is the mass of the beaker now?...

5.5 g of salt

6 Why is copper used in electrical wiring?
   Choose one answer.
   a) copper is shiny
   b) copper does not react with water
   c) copper is a good conductor of electricity.

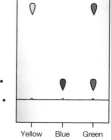

7. Three inks, yellow, blue and green, were compared using chromatography.
   a) Which ink is made of two substances?...
   b) Name the two colours this ink is made from..

Yellow   Blue   Green

8. The table below shows the melting and boiling temperatures of four halogens.

Element	Melting temperature °C	Boiling temperature °C
fluorine	−220	−188
chlorine	−101	−34
bromine	−7	59
iodine	114	184

Using the table name one substance which at room temperature is:
   a) a solid...
   b) a liquid..
   c) a gas...

9. A student heated some magnesium in a crucible.
   She did not lose any of the magnesium oxide that was formed.
   The mass of the crucible was measured before and after heating.

30.00 g	30.24 g	30.40 g
empty crucible	crucible and magnesium	crucible and magnesium oxide

   a) Write a word equation for the reaction.....................................
   b) Why has the mass of the contents increased during this reaction?
   ....

10. Iron oxide reacts with carbon monoxide to form iron and carbon dioxide.
    a) Name three compounds mentioned here...
    b) Name one element named here...

11. Limestone is mainly calcium carbonate. It decomposes on heating to form calcium oxide and the gas
    carbon dioxide.
    Write a word equation for this reaction..

12. Four metals were placed in solutions of different metal sulphate solutions. The results are shown in the
    table below. (If a reaction occurred a tick is shown, if no reaction took place a cross is shown.)

Metal	Magnesium sulphate	Copper sulphate solution	Iron sulphate solution	Zinc sulphate solution
magnesium	–	✓	✓	✓
copper	✗	–	✗	✗
iron	✗	✓	–	✗
zinc	✗	✓	✓	–

    a) Using the table write down the order of reactivity for these four metals. Write the most reactive metal first.

    ....

    b) Give a word equation for the reaction between magnesium and zinc sulphate.

    ....

13. Methane (natural gas) is burnt in Bunsen burners
    Complete a word equation for methane burning in plenty of oxygen.

    ....

14. The diagram shows a cross section of rock. T is a small igneous intrusion.
    a) Why are the crystals at T smaller than those at S?..
    b) Why are the metamorphic rocks at V different to the metamorphic
       rocks at U?..

How did you do?

1–3	correct	....start again
4–6	correct	....getting there
7–11	correct	....good work
12–14	correct	....excellent

SPEED

The <u>speed</u> of an object is a measure of <u>how</u> <u>fast</u> <u>it</u> <u>is</u> <u>moving</u>.

CALCULATING SPEEDS

To find the speed of an object we need to know <u>how</u> <u>far</u> <u>it</u> <u>has</u> <u>travelled</u> and <u>how</u> <u>long</u> <u>it</u> <u>took</u> to travel this distance. Then we use the equation.

$$\text{speed} = \frac{\text{distance}}{\text{time}} \quad \text{or} \quad s = \frac{d}{t}$$

EXAMPLE
Calculate the speed of a sprinter who runs 100 m in 10 s.

$$s = \frac{d}{t} = \frac{100 \text{ m}}{10 \text{ s}} = 10 \text{ m/s}$$

This answer tells us that the sprinter, on average, ran 10 m every second.

EXAMPLE
Calculate the speed of a car which travels 300 km in 5 hours.

$$s = \frac{d}{t} = \frac{300 \text{ km}}{5 \text{ h}} = 60 \text{ km/h}$$

The car, on average, travels 60 km each hour.

Examiner's Top Tip
Whenever you do a calculation be sure to write down the units of your answer. An answer of 10 to the above question may not have gained you full marks. An answer of 10 <u>m/s</u> will get you all the marks available.

SPEED AND VELOCITY

We often use the words <u>speed</u> and <u>velocity</u> as if they have the same meaning, but there is a small but important difference.
• A speed tells us how fast an object is moving.
• A velocity tells us how fast an object is moving <u>and</u> <u>in</u> <u>which</u> <u>direction</u>.
• 20 m/s is a speed. 20 m/s northwards is a velocity.

CALCULATING DISTANCES AND TIMES

Some questions may give you the speed of an object and ask you to calculate either:
a) the distance it travels in a certain time or
b) the time it takes to travel a certain distance.

Both of these are very easy to do once you know how to use the formula triangle. We draw the triangle with the letters in the same place as they are in the formula.
So $s = \dfrac{d}{t}$

is drawn in the formula triangle as:

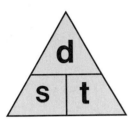

To find the formula to calculate the distance we simply cover the d in the triangle:

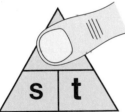

Now we can see that $d = s \times t$

EXAMPLE
A cannonball after being fired travels at 75 m/s for 4 s. How far has the ball travelled?
$d = s \times t = 75$ m/s $\times 4$ s $= 300$ m
To find the formula to calculate time we simply cover the t in the triangle

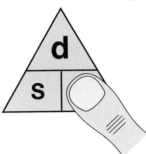

Now we can see that $t = \dfrac{d}{s}$

EXAMPLE
A cyclist travels 80 km at an average speed of 20 km/h. How long does the journey take?
$t = \dfrac{d}{s} = \dfrac{80 \text{ km}}{20 \text{ km/h}} = 4$ hours

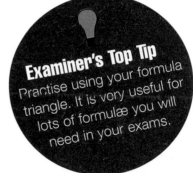
Examiner's Top Tip
Practise using your formula triangle. It is very useful for lots of formulæ you will need in your exams.

ACCELERATION

If an object is __speeding up__ it is __accelerating__. If an object is __slowing down__ it is __decelerating__.

QUICK TEST

1. What two measurements do you need to calculate the speed of an object?
2. Name two units you could use to measure the speed of an object.
3. Calculate the speed of a woman who runs 400 m in 80 s.
4. How long will it take a boy cycling at 20 m/s to travel 400 m?
5. How far will a bus travel in 5 hours if its speed is 60 km/h?

1. Distance travelled and time taken.
2. m/s and km/h
3. 5 m/s
4. 20 s
5. 300 km

GRAPHS OF MOTION

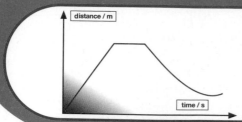

It is often useful to show the <u>journey of an object</u> in the form of a <u>graph</u>. There are two types of graph: <u>distance–time graphs</u> and <u>speed– or velocity–time graphs</u>.

Examiner's Top Tip
It is very easy in an exam to mix these graphs up. Before writing your answer, double-check the words next to the y-axis. Is it a distance–time graph or a velocity–time graph?

DISTANCE–TIME GRAPHS

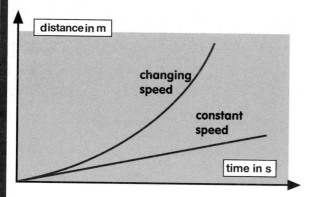

Horizontal line: object is <u>not moving</u>.

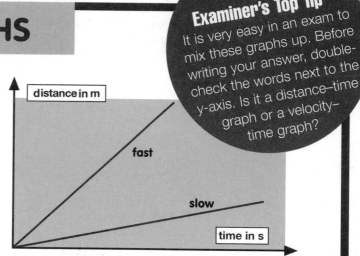

Sloping straight line: object moving at <u>constant speed</u>. Steeper straight line: object moving at a <u>greater constant speed</u>.

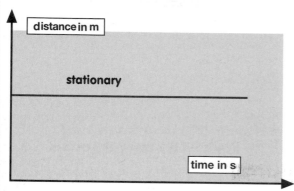

Steepness or gradient of line changes: speed of object is <u>not constant</u>.

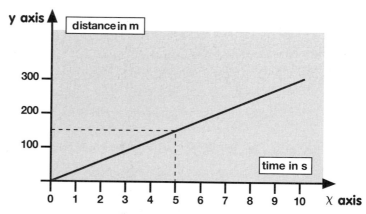

<u>Speed</u> of an object is equal to the <u>gradient of the line</u>.

Speed of object = $\dfrac{y}{x}$ = $\dfrac{150}{5}$ = 30 m/s

This example shows how a distance-time graph can be used to describe a journey.
A man walking at a constant speed travels 200m in 100 s. He then stops for 150s. He completes the final leg of his journey travelling 100m in 50s.

distance-time graph for this journey

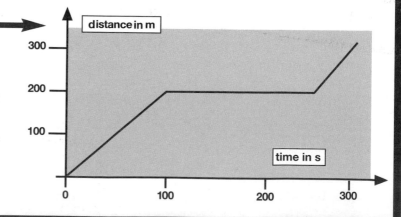

SPEED– OR VELOCITY–TIME GRAPHS

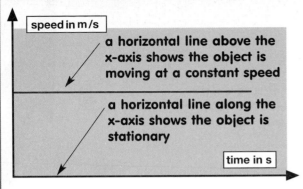

A <u>horizontal</u> <u>line</u> along the axis shows the object is <u>stationary</u>.
A <u>horizontal</u> <u>line</u> above the axis shows the object is moving at <u>constant</u> <u>speed</u>.

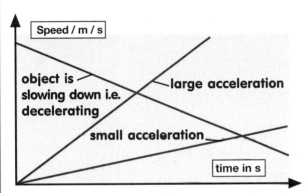

A line sloping upwards: shows the object is increasing its speed, i.e. <u>accelerating</u>
A line sloping downwards: shows the object decreasing its speed, i.e. <u>decelerating</u>
The <u>steeper</u> <u>the</u> <u>line</u> the <u>greater</u> <u>the</u> <u>acceleration</u> <u>or</u> <u>deceleration</u> of the object.

EXAMPLE

The example below shows how a speed time graph can be used to describe the journey of a motorist.
A motorist starting from rest accelerates to a speed of 40 m/s in 4 s. She travels at this speed for 10 s before decelerating to a halt in 8 s.

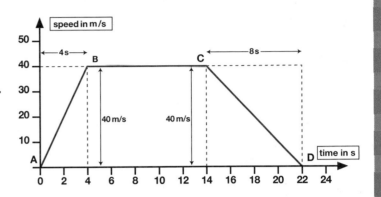

Examiner's Top Tip
If you have to draw a graph remember to:
• use a sharp pencil and don't press too hard. You may want to rub it out!
• use a ruler for straight lines and axises
• label the axises and include units.

QUICK TEST

1. On a distance–time graph what do the following show?
   a) a horizontal line
   b) a steeply sloping straight line
   c) a straight line sloping just a little.

2. On a speed–time graph what do the following show?
   a) a horizontal line
   b) a straight line sloping steeply upwards
   c) a straight line sloping gently downwards.

1. a) a stationary object
   b) large constant speed
   c) small constant speed
2. a) constant speed
   b) large acceleration
   c) small deceleration

EFFECTS OF FORCES ON OBJECTS

When forces like these are applied to an object they may cause an object to:

- start moving if it is stationary

- stop moving if it is already moving

- speed it up

- slow it down

- change its direction.

Sometimes a force can be applied to an object without any physical contact.

This diver is being pulled downwards by a force we call gravity. The size of this gravitational attraction we call <u>weight</u>.

These objects are being attracted by the magnet.

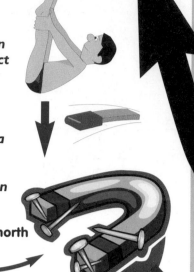

north

south

MEASURING FORCES

We can measure the size of a force using a <u>newtonmeter</u>. This consists of a a spring and a scale; the scale measures how much the spring stretches when a force is applied to it. The larger the force the more the spring extends. We measure forces in <u>newtons</u> (N). An average-sized apple has a weight of about 1 N.

newtometer

0N
1N
2N
3N
4N
5N

FORCES AND ACCELERATION

An object whose motion is changing is <u>accelerating</u>. The size of the acceleration depends on
- The size of the force....The larger the force the greater the acceleration for the <u>same</u> mass.
- The mass of the object....The larger the mass the smaller the acceleration for the <u>same</u> force.

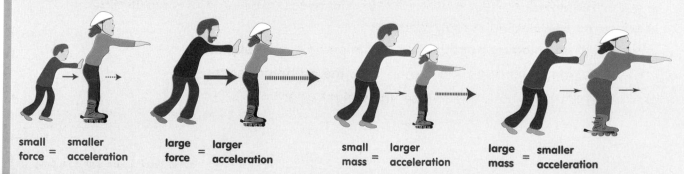

small force = smaller acceleration

large force = larger acceleration

small mass = larger acceleration

large mass = smaller acceleration

BALANCED FORCES

If several forces are applied to an object, they may <u>cancel</u> <u>each</u> <u>other</u> <u>out</u>. The forces are <u>balanced</u>.

· If the forces applied to an object are <u>balanced</u> they will have <u>no</u> <u>effect</u> <u>on</u> <u>its</u> <u>motion</u>.

· If the object is stationary it will <u>remain</u> <u>stationary</u>.

balanced forces: no motion

upward force due to bent branch

stationary object

weight

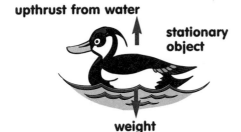

upthrust from water

stationary object

weight

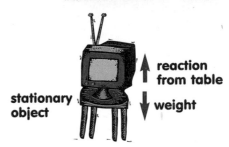

reaction from table

stationary object

weight

· If the object is moving it will <u>continue</u> <u>to</u> <u>move</u> <u>in</u> <u>the</u> <u>same</u> <u>direction</u> and at the <u>same</u> <u>speed</u>.

If the driving force of this aircraft equals the drag, it will travel at a constant speed. If the lift force equals the weight, the aircraft will stay at a constant height.

drag (or air resistance)

lift

driving force

weight

FORCES

Examiner's Top Tip
Remember: balanced forces mean no change to speed or direction, unbalanced forces cause change.

UNBALANCED FORCES

• If the forces applied to an object do not cancel each other out, i.e. they are <u>unbalanced</u>, they will affect its motion.

Stationary object made to move. Unbalanced forces.

QUICK TEST

1. Name three possible effects of applying a force to an object.

2. Name two forces that can be applied to an object without any physical contact.

3. What do we measure with a newtonmeter?

4. What effect do balanced forces have on the motion of an object?

5. What effect may unbalanced forces have on the motion of an object?

6. Explain what is meant by the phrase 'the weight of the object is 10 N'?

6. The pull of gravity on the object is 10 N.
5. Change direction, change speed
4. No effect.
3. The size of a force.
2. Magnetic and gravitational forces.
1. It may speed up, slow down, change direction or change shape.

FRICTION AND AIR RESISTANCE

FRICTION

Whenever an object moves or tries to move, <u>friction</u> is present.

Friction is present when:
- Two surfaces are gripping. This is called <u>static friction</u>.
- Two surfaces are sliding over each other. This is called <u>sliding friction</u>.

friction acts in the direction that opposes the motion

Friction between the tyres of a car and the surface of a road is very important. If there is insufficient grip it is impossible to stop or steer the car safely.

REDUCING FRICTION BY STREAMLINING AND LUBRICATING

- As this bobsleigh travels down the run it gains speed.
- There are then large frictional forces between the sleigh and the air and between the runners and the ice.
- To keep these forces to a minimum the bobsleigh is:
  a) streamlined. It is shaped so it cuts through the air with less resistance.
  b) the runners are coated with a lubricant, such as wax.

MOVING THROUGH AIR

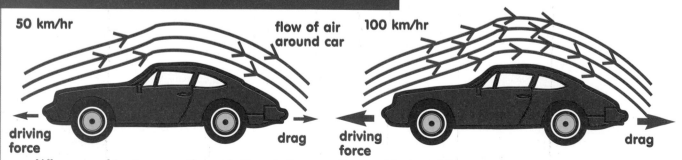

50 km/hr

flow of air around car

100 km/hr

driving force

drag

driving force

drag

- *When an object moves through the air it experiences <u>frictional forces</u>.*
- *These frictional forces are called <u>air resistance</u> or <u>drag</u> and try to prevent the object's motion.*
- *The <u>faster</u> the object moves the <u>larger</u> these resistive forces become.*

TERMINAL VELOCITY: CARS

Action	Result
Driver begins journey by pressing accelerator.	The driving force from the engine makes the car accelerate.
Accelerator is kept in same position.	As the speed of the car increases the air resistance increases. The car will have a smaller acceleration.
Accelerator is kept in same position.	The air resistance and the driving force are equal and balanced. The car travels at a constant speed called its terminal velocity.

driving force

driving force — air resistance

driving force — air resistance

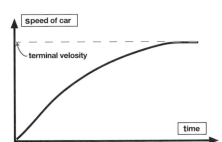
speed of car
terminal velosity
time

Examiner's Top Tip
Remember streamlining and lubricating reduce friction. Rough surfaces and high speeds increase friction.

EFFECTS OF FRICTION

friction between surfaces can wear them away

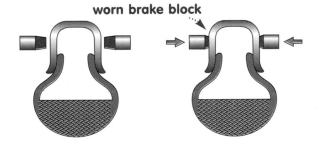
worn brake block

friction between surfaces can make them hot

QUICK TEST

1. In which direction does friction act?
2. What is streamlining?
3. What is a lubricant?
4. Name one situation where the presence of friction is an advantage.
5. What happens to a moving object if the driving force and the resistive forces are balanced?
6. Friction can cause .... and ....

1. Opposite direction to motion.
2. Shaping to reduce air resistance.
3. Substance used to reduce friction between surfaces.
4. Striking a match.
5. Constant velocity.
6. Wear and heat.

MOMENTS

- Forces sometimes make objects <u>turn or rotate</u>.
- The <u>turning effect of a force</u> is called a <u>moment</u>.
- You created a moment with your fingers when you opened this book.

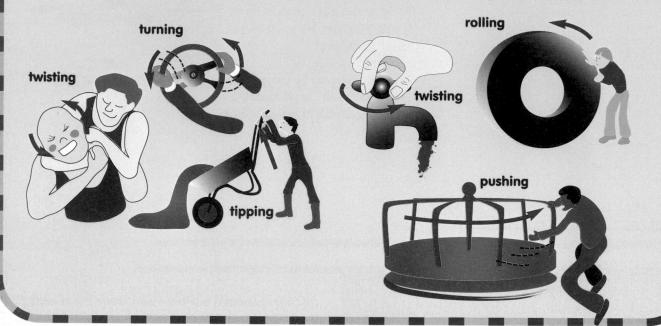

turning

twisting

tipping

rolling

twisting

pushing

THE SIZE OF A MOMENT

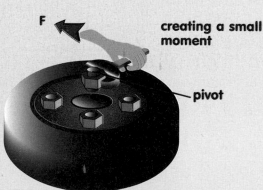

F   creating a small moment

pivot

F   creating a larger moment

pivot

- This moment is trying to undo a nut. The point the spanner will turn around is called <u>the pivot</u>

- If the nut is too stiff we can increase the size of the moment by:

a) using a longer spanner or

b) applying a bigger force to the spanner.

- The size of a moment can be calculated using the equation:

We measure moments in Nm.

100 N

pivot

0.5 m

- The moment being applied to this spanner is 100 N x 0.5 m = 50 Nm

<u>moment of a force</u> = <u>force</u> x <u>perpendicular distance of force from pivot</u>

BALANCING MOMENTS

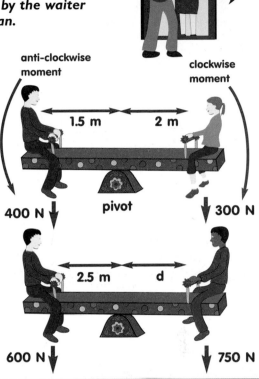

- If <u>two</u> <u>equal</u> <u>and</u> <u>opposite</u> <u>moments</u> are applied to an object there will be <u>no</u> turning: the moments are balanced.
- In the opposite diagram, the anticlockwise moments created by the waiter are balanced by the clockwise moments created by the woman.
- When balanced:

<u>clockwise</u> <u>moments</u> = <u>anticlockwise</u> <u>moments</u>
(known as the Principle of Moments.)

If this see-saw balances, the clockwise moments created by the girl must be equal to the anticlockwise moments created by the boy.
300 x 2 = 400 x 1.5 m

EXAMPLE
A boy weighing 600 N sits 2.5 m from the centre of a see-saw. How far from the centre of the see-saw should his friend sit so that the see-saw balances? His friend weighs 750 N.

- If the see-saw balances:
<u>clockwise</u> <u>moments</u> = <u>anticlockwise</u> <u>moments</u>
750 N x d = 600 N x 2.5 m
$d = \dfrac{600 \text{ N} \times 2.5 \text{ m}}{750 \text{ N}}$
d = 2.0m

anti-clockwise moment

clockwise moment

1.5 m   2 m

400 N   pivot   300 N

2.5 m   d

600 N   750 N

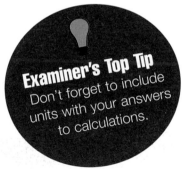

Key Terms
Make sure you understand these terms before moving on:
- moment
- pivot
- perpendicular distance
- clockwise and anticlockwise moments

QUICK TEST

1. What is a moment?
2. A force of 200 N is applied perpendicular to and at the end of a spanner 0.4 m long. Calculate the moment created by the force.
3. Suggest two ways in which you could increase the moment applied by the spanner.
4. Under what conditions will two moments applied to the same object balance?
5. A man weighing 1200 N sits 1.5 m to the left of the centre of a see-saw. His friend weighs 1100 N and sits on the opposite side, 1.8 m from the centre. Why does the see-saw not balance?
6. Which way does the seesaw in question 5 turn?

6. Clockwise
5. Clockwise moments do not equal anticlockwise moments.
4. Clockwise moments = anticlockwise moments.
3. Apply a larger force same force and apply at point further from pivot.
2. 80 Nm
1. Turning effect of a force defined as force x perpendicular distance.

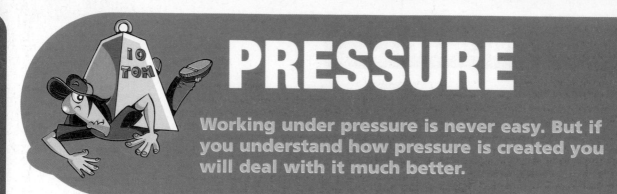

PRESSURE

Working under pressure is never easy. But if you understand how pressure is created you will deal with it much better.

WHAT IS PRESSURE?

Pressure is a measure of how <u>concentrated</u> or <u>spread out</u> a force is.

- If a force is applied over a <u>small area</u> it creates a <u>large pressure</u>.

- If the force is applied over a <u>large area</u> it creates a <u>small pressure</u>.

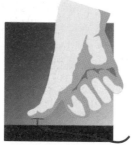

force over small area

If a knife is sharp the pressure under its blade is high and cutting the cheese is easy. If the blade is blunt the pressure would be lower and cutting the cheese much more difficult.

If the handles of a carrier bag are thin they can create an uncomfortably high pressure on your hands.

Camels have large feet to prevent them from sinking into the sand.

If all your weight is concentrated a small area the pressure created can be very painful.

CALCULATING PRESSURE

We can calculate the pressure created by a force using the equation:

pressure = $\frac{force}{area}$ or $P = \frac{F}{A}$

- We measure pressure in _pascals (Pa)_. Where 1 Pa = 1 N/m²

EXAMPLE

A crate weighing 1000 N is standing upright on one of its sides which measures 2 m x 2 m. Calculate the pressure created on the ground by the crate.

$P = \frac{F}{A} = \frac{1000}{4}$ N/m² = 250 Pa

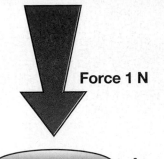

Force 1 N

Area 1 m²

pressure = 1 Pa

Force 100 N

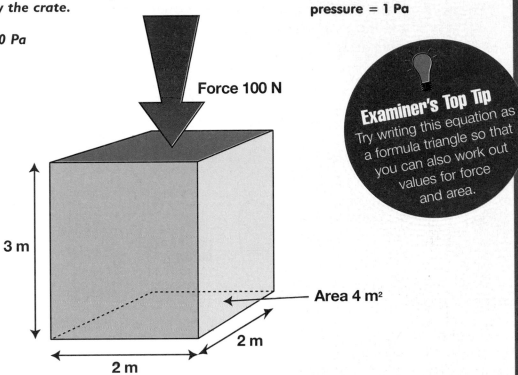

3 m

Area 4 m²

2 m

2 m

Examiner's Top Tip
Try writing this equation as a formula triangle so that you can also work out values for force and area.

QUICK TEST

1. How do we create a high pressure?

2. How can we avoid or reduce a high pressure?

3. Why are full carrier bags sometimes painful to carry?

4. In what units do we measure pressure?

5. Why does a sharp knife cut through a piece of cheese easier than a blunt knife?

6. Calculate the pressure created when a force of 50 N is over an area of 2.5 m².

7. Calculate the pressure created when a crate weighing 4000 N is standing on the side of the crate measuring 4 m x 2 m.

8. Draw a formula triangle for the equation $P = \frac{F}{A}$

9. What force when applied to an area of 2 m² will create a pressure of 40 Pa?

9. 80 N

8.

7. 500 Pa

6. 20 Pa

5. Greater pressure under blade

4. Pascal (Pa)

3. Weight of contents concentrated over very small area.

2. Spread the force over a large area.

1. Large force over a small area.

LIGHT RAYS AND REFLECTION
Light travels in <u>straight</u> <u>lines</u>.

SEEING OBJECTS

- We see <u>luminous</u> <u>objects</u> such as fires, light bulbs and stars because some of the light they <u>emit</u> enters our eyes.
- We see non-luminous objects because some of the light they <u>reflect</u> enters our eyes.

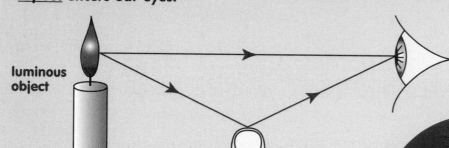

luminous object

non-luminous object

Examiner's Top Tip
Always put arrowheads on rays. If the ray changes direction, put one arrow-head on the ray before the change and one after.

Examiner's Top Tip
Angles are always measured between the ray and the normal. A normal is a line at 90° to the surface.

SHADOWS

- We can see through a <u>transparent</u> object, e.g. a pane of glass, because the light <u>can</u> <u>pass</u> through it.
- We can not see through an <u>opaque</u> object, e.g. a piece of wood, because the light <u>cannot</u> <u>pass</u> through it.
- An opaque object placed in front of a source of light will create <u>a shadow</u>.
- A shadow is a dark area where there is <u>little</u> <u>or</u> <u>no light</u>.
- The shadow will have the <u>same shape</u> as the object creating it.
- This is because light travels in straight lines.

Examiner's Top Tip
Always draw ray diagrams using a ruler and pencil. Be neat!

THE SPEED OF LIGHT

- Light travels very quickly.
- Over short distances it seems to be there <u>almost</u> <u>instantaneously</u>.
- It takes light just eight minutes to travel from the Sun to the Earth.
- It travels at a speed of <u>300</u> <u>million</u> <u>metres</u> a second.

- Sound travels at a speed of just 340 m a second.
- Because light travels much more quickly there is sometimes a <u>delay</u> between <u>seeing</u> <u>and</u> <u>hearing</u>.
- The fireworks in the diagram are seen to explode but then there is a delay of several seconds before we hear the explosion.

REFLECTION FROM A PLANE MIRROR

- When a ray of light strikes a plane mirror it is reflected so that the <u>angle</u> <u>of</u> <u>incidence</u> is equal to the <u>angle</u> <u>of</u> <u>reflection</u>. The angles are always measured from the normal.

angle i = angle r

normal

incident ray

i   r   reflected ray

plane mirror

SIMPLE PERISCOPE

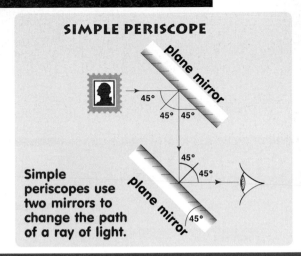

plane mirror

45°

45° 45°

45°

45°

plane mirror

45°

Simple periscopes use two mirrors to change the path of a ray of light.

PLANE AND DIFFUSION REFLECTION

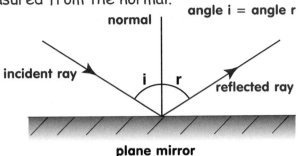

shiny surface   matt or rough surface

- **All the rays are reflected in the same direction. Lots of light enters our eyes so the surface looks <u>shiny</u> or <u>glossy</u>.**

- **Because the light is <u>scattered</u>, only a little of it enters our eyes so the surface appears <u>dull</u> or <u>matt</u>.**

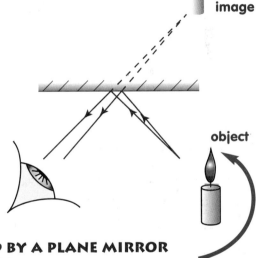

virtual image

object

THE IMAGE CREATED BY A PLANE MIRROR
The image of an object is:
- <u>upright</u>
- the <u>same</u> <u>size</u> as the object
- the <u>same</u> <u>distance</u> behind the mirror as the object is in front
- <u>laterally</u> <u>inverted</u>, i.e. the left is on the right and the right is on the left
- a <u>virtual</u> <u>image</u>, i.e. it cannot be formed on a screen placed behind the mirror.

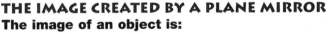

QUICK TEST

1. How do we know light travels in straight lines?

2. What is an opaque object?

3. What is a transparent object?

4. What is a luminous object?

5. How do we see a non-luminous object?

6. The angle of incidence is equal to ....

7. Describe the image that is created by a plane mirror.

1. Shadows are the same shape as the object.
2. One which light cannot pass through.
3. One which is see-through.
4. One which gives off its own light.
5. By the light it reflects.
6. The angle of reflection.
7. Upright, same size, same distance behind mirror and laterally inverted.

REFRACTION AND COLOUR

REFRACTION

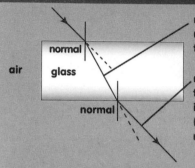

ray bends towards normal as it enters the glass

ray bends away from the normal as it leaves the block (parallel to original ray).

air

normal

glass

normal

- When a ray of light enters a glass block, it slows down and bends towards the normal.
- This change of direction is called refraction.
- When the ray emerges from the block, it speeds up and bends away from the normal.
- But if the ray meets the surface at 90° it is not refracted.

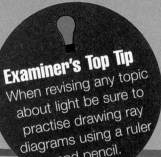

no refraction at either surface

Examiner's Top Tip
When revising any topic about light be sure to practise drawing ray diagrams using a ruler and pencil.

STRANGE EFFECTS OF REFRACTION
This pencil looks bent because the rays of light are refracted as they emerge from the water. This swimming pool is deeper than it appears. This is also caused by refraction.

pencil

water

beaker

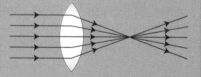

apparent depth of swimming pool

air

ray is refracted

water

i

o

real depth of swimming pool

LENSES
Lenses are specially shaped pieces of glass or plastic, which are used to refract light in a particular direction.

- A converging lens refracts the light so that rays of light are brought together (converge).

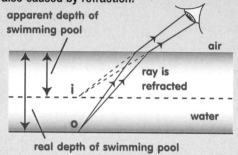

- A diverging lens refracts light so that rays of light are made to spread out or diverge.

Key Terms
Make sure you understand these terms before moving on:
- Dispersion
- Spectrum
- Dye
- Coloured filter
- Total internal reflection
- Optical fibre

DISPERSION

- **White light is a <u>mixture</u> <u>of</u> <u>coloured</u> <u>lights</u>.**
- **When white light travels through a <u>prism</u>, the different colours are <u>refracted</u> by different amounts. This is called <u>dispersion</u>.**
- **A <u>band</u> <u>of</u> <u>colours</u> called a <u>spectrum</u> is produced.**
- **The colours of the spectrum are always in the same order: <u>r</u>ed, <u>o</u>range, <u>y</u>ellow, green, <u>b</u>lue, <u>i</u>ndigo and <u>v</u>iolet.**

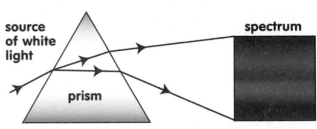

Easy to remember: Richard Of York Gave Battle In Vain.

COLOURED OBJECTS

- **Coloured objects contain a chemical called a <u>dye</u>.**
- **When white lights hits a coloured object all the colours of the spectrum are <u>absorbed</u> by the dye <u>except</u> <u>for</u> <u>its</u> <u>own</u> <u>colour</u>. This is reflected into the eye of the observer.**
- **White objects reflect all colours.**
- **Black objects reflect no light.**

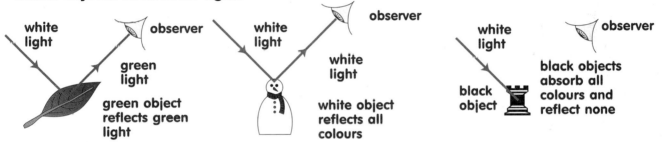

COLOURED FILTERS

<u>Filters</u> **are <u>coloured</u> <u>pieces</u> <u>of</u> <u>transparent</u> <u>plastic</u> <u>or</u> <u>glass</u> which <u>only</u> <u>allow</u> <u>light</u> <u>of</u> <u>the</u> <u>same</u> <u>colour</u> <u>to</u> <u>pass</u> <u>through</u>. For example, green light can pass through a green filter but red or blue light will be absorbed.**

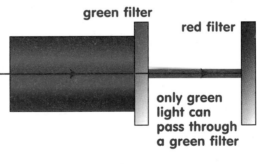

QUICK TEST

1. What is the bending of a ray of light as it enters a glass block called?

2. Which way does a ray bend as it travels from air into glass?

3. Name one device that makes use of refraction.

4. What is a spectrum?

5. How is a spectrum produced?

6. Explain how an observer sees a green object in white light.

7. What is a green filter?

7. Transparent plastic that only allows green light through.
6. Only green light is reflected.
5. Dispersion
4. Band of colours
3. A lens
2. Towards the normal
1. Refraction

SOUNDS

All sounds begin with an <u>object</u> that is <u>vibrating</u>. These vibrations travel outwards from the source. If they strike someone's <u>eardrum</u>, they may be heard.

PITCH AND FREQUENCY

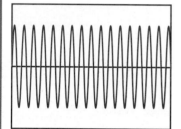

low pitched sound

- Large objects <u>vibrate</u> <u>slowly</u> and produce just a few waves each second. These waves have a <u>low</u> <u>frequency</u> and produce <u>low</u> <u>pitched</u> <u>sounds</u>.

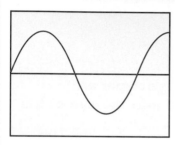

high pitched sound

- Small objects vibrate quickly and produce lots of waves each second. These waves have a <u>high</u> <u>frequency</u> and produce <u>high</u> <u>pitched</u> <u>sounds</u>.
- We measure the <u>frequency</u> of a wave or its source in <u>hertz</u> (<u>Hz</u>). An object which <u>vibrates</u> <u>once</u> <u>every</u> <u>second</u> and produces <u>one</u> <u>complete</u> <u>wave</u> <u>every</u> <u>second</u> has a <u>frequency</u> <u>of</u> <u>1</u> <u>Hz</u>.

LOUDNESS

- **Objects that vibrate with <u>large amplitudes</u> produce <u>loud</u> <u>sounds</u>.**
- **Objects that have <u>small vibrations</u> produce <u>quiet</u> <u>sounds</u>.**

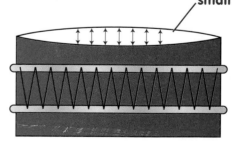

drum skin — large vibrations

drum

small vibrations

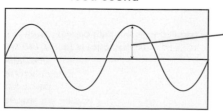

loud sound — large amplitude

quiet sound — small amplitude

TRAVELLING SOUND WAVES

My sound wave's are travelling through the string to you.

- Although we normally think of sound waves as travelling through air they can travel through all solids, liquids and gases. Sound waves travel by making particles vibrate
- There are no particles in a vacuum therefore: <u>sound</u> <u>waves</u> <u>cannot</u> <u>travel</u> <u>through</u> <u>a</u> <u>vacuum</u>.

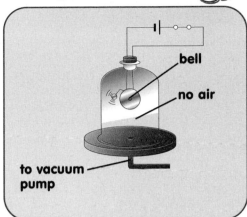

bell

no air

to vacuum pump

- When the bell is turned on we can see and hear it ring.
- When all the air has been sucked out of the jar by the vacuum pump we can see that the bell is still ringing but we can not hear it
- Conclusion: Light waves can travel through a vacuum but sound waves cannot.
- Sound waves travel much more slowly than light waves. This is why we often see an event before we hear it. e.g. thunder and lightning.

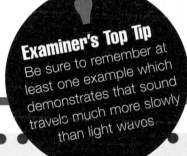

Examiner's Top Tip
Be sure to remember at least one example which demonstrates that sound travels much more slowly than light waves

QUICK TEST

1. All sounds begin with an object, which is ....
2. A large object will produce a .... sound
3. A small object will produce a .... sound
4. Loud sounds are produced by objects with large .... of vibration.
5. Through what can a sound wave not travel? Explain your answer.
6. Why do we see lightning before we hear the thunder?

6. Light waves travel much faster than sound waves.
5. A vacuum. It contains no particles to vibrate.
4. Amplitudes
3. High-pitched
2. Low-pitched
1. Vibrating

ECHOES AND HEARING

ECHOES

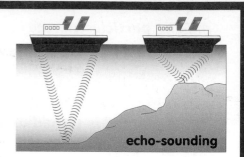

echo-sounding

- When sound waves strike a hard surface they are <u>reflected</u>. This reflected sound is called an <u>echo</u>.
- Ships use echoes to find the depth of the ocean beneath them. An <u>echo-sounder</u> emits sound waves down towards the seabed. When the waves strike the seabed, they are reflected back up to the surface. A sound detector 'listens' for the echo.
- The deeper the ocean the longer it is before the echo is heard. Sound waves used in this way are called <u>SONAR</u>. This stands for <u>SO</u>und <u>N</u>avigation <u>A</u>nd <u>R</u>anging.
- Fishing boats often use sonar to detect shoals of fish. If an echo is heard sooner than expected it is likely that the wave has been reflected from a shoal of fish swimming beneath the boat.

HEARING RANGE (SOMETIMES CALLED AUDIBLE RANGE)

- An average person can only hear sounds that have a frequency above 20 Hz but below 20 000 Hz. This band of frequencies is called our <u>hearing range</u>.
- Hearing ranges do vary slightly from person to person but in general as we get older our hearing range becomes narrower.
- Sounds that have a frequency which is too high for the human ear to detect are called <u>ultrasounds</u>.

- Ultrasounds can be heard by some animals.
- <u>Dog whistles</u> produce notes we can not detect but can be heard by a dog.

Examiner's Top Tip
Don't try to memorise any of the figures from this section but do try to understand that different people have different hearing ranges and that loud sounds can cause permanent hearing problems.

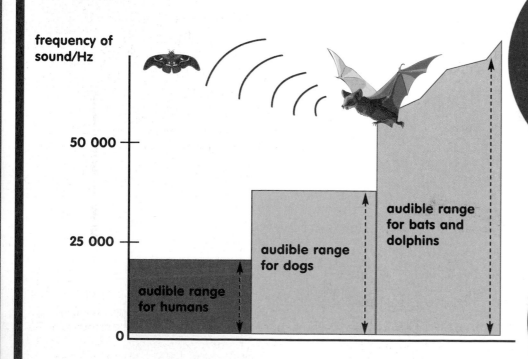

frequency of sound/Hz

50 000

25 000

0

audible range for humans

audible range for dogs

audible range for bats and dolphins

Examiner's Top Tip
When you read an exam question look at the number of marks it is worth. If it is worth three marks try to write three facts.

LOUDNESS AND THE DECIBEL SCALE

- Constant exposure to loud sounds can <u>damage</u> <u>your</u> <u>hearing</u>.
- People who work with noisy machinery should wear <u>ear</u> <u>defenders</u> to protect their hearing.
- People listening to music through earphones should be careful not to have the volume turned up too high. The <u>damage</u> caused to their hearing by persistent exposure to loud sounds could be permanent.

- We measure loudness on the <u>decibel</u> <u>scale</u>.

dB
140
130
120
110
100
90
80
70
60
50
40
30
20
10
0

Key Terms

Make sure you understand the following terms before moving on:

- Echo
- Sonar
- Hearing range
- Ultrasounds
- Loudness
- Decibel scale

QUICK TEST

1. What is an echo?
2. What is the hearing range of an average person?
3. What is an ultrasound?
4. Name two animals that can hear ultrasounds.
5. How can workers avoid damage to their hearing if they use noisy machinery in their work?
6. How can you avoid damaging your hearing when listening to your personal stereo?

1. Reflection of a sound wave
2. 20 Hz to 20 000 Hz
3. Frequency too high for humans to hear.
4. Dogs, bats
5. Ear defenders
6. Turn down the volume.

ENERGY

We all need <u>energy</u> in order <u>to be able</u> <u>to do things</u>. As human beings we get this energy from the food we eat. <u>Food</u> is a form of <u>chemical</u> energy. But there are other forms of energy.

DIFFERENT FORMS OF ENERGY

HEAT OR THERMAL ENERGY
Hot objects are sources of <u>heat</u> energy.

LIGHT ENERGY
The Sun, light bulbs and lamps are luminous objects. They give off <u>light</u> energy.

SOUND ENERGY
Vibrating objects give off <u>sound</u> energy.

ELECTRICAL ENERGY
<u>Electrical</u> energy is available every time a current flows. The electrical energy from this battery is being used to make the bulb glow.

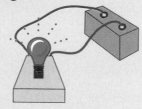

CHEMICAL ENERGY
Food, fuels and batteries all contain <u>chemical</u> energy.

KINETIC ENERGY
This is the energy an object has because it is moving.
Wind (moving air) and flowing water have <u>kinetic</u> energy.

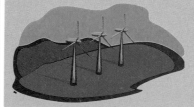

ELASTIC POTENTIAL ENERGY
Objects such as springs and rubber bands that are stretched or twisted or bent contain <u>elastic</u> <u>potential</u> energy.

GRAVITATIONAL POTENTIAL ENERGY
Objects that have a high position and are able to fall have <u>gravitational</u> <u>potential</u> energy.

NUCLEAR ENERGY
Reactions in the centre or nucleus of an atom are the source of <u>nuclear</u> energy.

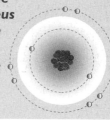

STORED ENERGY
- Chemical energy, elastic potential energy and gravitational potential energy are often referred to as forms of <u>stored</u> energy.
- They are forms of energy that are <u>waiting</u> <u>to be used</u>.

chemical energy in the wax

ENERGY TRANSFERS

When energy is used <u>it</u> <u>does</u> <u>not</u> <u>disappear</u>. It is <u>transferred</u> <u>into</u> <u>other</u> <u>different</u> <u>forms</u> of energy.

A <u>light</u> <u>bulb</u> changes <u>electrical</u> <u>energy</u> into <u>heat</u> <u>and</u> <u>light</u> <u>energy</u>.

A <u>log</u> <u>fire</u> changes <u>chemical</u> <u>energy</u> into <u>heat</u> <u>and</u> <u>light</u> <u>energy</u>.

A <u>loudspeaker</u> changes <u>electrical</u> <u>energy</u> into <u>sound</u>.

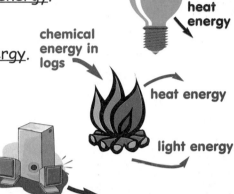

Other examples of energy changes:

Energy in	Energy changer	Energy out
Chemical (food)	Animal	Heat, kinetic, chemical
Light	Solar cell	Electrical
Kinetic	Wind turbine	Electrical
Strain potential energy	Bow and arrow	Kinetic
Chemical	Battery	Electrical
Electrical	Battery charger	Chemical
Sound	Microphone	Electrical
Electrical	Electric motor	Kinetic
Kinetic energy	Generator	Electrical
Gravitational potential energy	Falling object	Kinetic
Elastic potential energy	Clockwork car	Kinetic

QUICK TEST

1. Name five different types of energy.
2. Name three types of stored energy.
3. What kind of energy does a crate gain as it is lifted by a crane?
4. What kind of energy does water gain as it travels down a waterfall?
5. Write down the energy transfer that takes place when using a hair drier.
6. Write down the energy transfer that takes place when you speak into a microphone.

6. Sound to electrical energy.
5. Electrical to heat, kinetic and sound.
4. Kinetic energy.
3. Gravitational potential energy.
2. Chemical, elastic and gravitational potential energy.
1. Heat, light, sound, electricity, chemical.

USING ENERGY RESOURCES

electrical energy ⇒ sound

Electricical energy is one of the <u>most</u> <u>convenient</u> <u>forms</u> <u>of</u> <u>energy</u>. It is <u>easily</u> <u>converted</u> into other forms of energy.

FOSSIL FUELS

Coal, oil and gas are called <u>fossil</u> <u>fuels</u>. They are <u>concentrated</u> <u>sources</u> of energy.

- Fossil fuels are formed from <u>plants</u> <u>and</u> <u>animals</u> that died over 100 million years ago.
- When they died they became <u>covered</u> <u>with</u> <u>many</u> <u>layers</u> <u>of</u> <u>mud</u> <u>and</u> <u>earth</u>.
- The resulting <u>large</u> <u>pressures</u> <u>and</u> <u>high</u> <u>temperatures</u> <u>changed</u> <u>them</u> <u>into</u> <u>fossil</u> <u>fuels</u>.
- Because they take <u>millions</u> <u>of</u> <u>years</u> <u>to</u> <u>form</u> these fuels are called <u>non-renewable</u> <u>fuels</u>.
- Once they have been used up they <u>cannot</u> <u>be</u> <u>replaced</u>.

Dead plants and animals being covered with mud and earth.

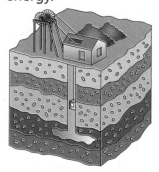

After hundreds of millions of years they have changed into fossil fuels such as coal.

THE PROBLEMS WITH NON-RENEWABLE FUELS
- When any of the fossil fuels are burned they produce <u>carbon</u> <u>dioxide</u>. Increasing the amount of carbon dioxide in the atmosphere will cause the temperature of the Earth and its atmosphere to rise. This is called the Greenhouse Effect.
- When coal and oil are burned they also produce gases that cause <u>acid</u> <u>rain</u>.
- <u>Environmental</u> <u>problems</u> are created by <u>mining</u> and <u>spillage</u> <u>of</u> <u>oil</u> <u>during</u> <u>transport</u>.
- We are using fossil fuels up very quickly and will soon have to find other sources of energy but we need to start looking <u>now</u>.

THE SOLUTIONS
- We need to slow down the rate at which we are using fossil fuels so that they will last longer. There are several ways in which we can do this.
- <u>Reduce petrol consumption</u> by driving smaller cars, using public transport or walking or cycling. We should also develop more efficient car engines.
- <u>Improve the insulation</u> to our homes and factories so less energy is wasted heating them.
- <u>Increase public awareness</u> of how people are wasting energy so that they turn off lights and turn down heating where possible.

- We need to make greater use of other sources of energy.
- In the UK some of our electricity is generated by <u>nuclear power stations</u>.
- <u>Renewable sources of energy</u> such as wind, waves, tidal, solar, geothermal, biomass and hydroelectric <u>need to be developed</u>. Each of these sources have some advantages and disadvantages. These are described in more detail on pages (110-111).

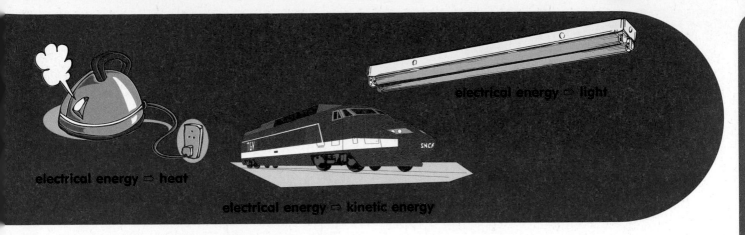

electrical energy ⇨ light

electrical energy ⇨ heat

electrical energy ⇨ kinetic energy

POWER STATIONS

Most of the electrical energy we use at home is generated at <u>power</u> <u>stations</u>. There are several different types of power station but the most common in the UK use <u>coal or gas as</u> <u>their</u> <u>source</u> <u>of</u> <u>energy</u> (<u>fuel</u>).

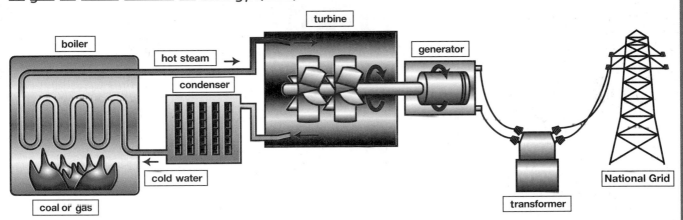

CHEMICAL ENERGY ➡➡ HEAT ENERGY ➡➡ KINETIC ENERGY ➡➡ ELECTRICAL ENERGY

- The fuel is burned to release its <u>chemical energy</u>.
- The <u>heat</u> <u>energy</u> <u>released</u> is used to heat water and turn it into <u>steam</u>.
- The steam <u>turns</u> <u>turbines</u>.
- The turbines <u>turn</u> <u>large</u> <u>generators</u>.
- The <u>generators</u> <u>produce</u> <u>electrical</u> <u>energy</u>.
- The electrical energy is carried to our homes through the <u>National Grid</u>.

Examiner's Top Tip
This is another very popular topic and appears regularly on exam papers. Make sure that you understand the energy changes that take place when electricity is generated at the power station. Also learn the problems that burning fossil fuels create for the atmosphere and the environment.

QUICK TEST

1. Name three fossil fuels.

2. What gas causes the greenhouse effect?

3. Which fossil fuels when burned cause acid rain?

4. Name one type of environmental damage that might be caused as a result of using fossil fuels in our power stations.

5. Why are fossil fuels called non-renewable sources of energy?

6. Suggest three ways in which we could make fossil fuels last longer.

6. More efficient insulation and engines. Make more use of alternative sources of energy.
5. Cannot be replaced.
4. Oil spillage.
3. Coal and oil.
2. Carbon dioxide.
1. Coal, oil and gas.

GEOTHERMAL

In regions where the Earth's crust is thin, <u>hot rocks beneath the ground</u> can be used to heat water turning it into steam. This steam is then used to drive turbines and generate electricity.

+ <u>Renewable</u> source of energy.
+ No pollution and no environmental problems.

– Very few <u>suitable sites</u>.
– <u>High</u> cost of drilling deep into the ground.

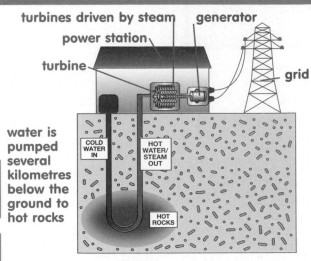

turbines driven by steam   generator
power station
turbine   grid

water is pumped several kilometres below the ground to hot rocks

COLD WATER IN   HOT WATER/ STEAM OUT

HOT ROCKS

radioactive decay produces heat to warm the rocks and magma chambers close to the surface.

ALTERNATIVE SOURCES OF ENERGY

+ = advantages   – = disadvantages

The energy carried in the Sun's rays is converted directly into electrical energy by solar cells. This then powers the car.

TIDAL POWER

At high tide, water is trapped behind a barrage or dam. When it is released at low tide the <u>gravitational potential energy of the water</u> changes into kinetic energy which then drives turbines and generates electricity.

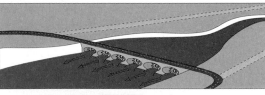

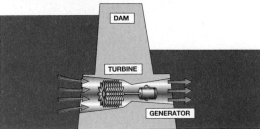

DAM

TURBINE

GENERATOR

+ <u>Renewable</u> source.
+ <u>Reliable</u>: two tides per day.
+ <u>No</u> atmospheric pollution.
+ <u>Low</u> running costs.

– <u>High</u> initial cost.
– Possible damage to environment, e.g. flooding.
– Obstacle to <u>water transport</u>.

SOLAR ENERGY

The energy carried in the <u>Sun's rays</u> can be converted directly into electricity using solar cells.

sunlight   electric current

solar cell

electrical components

OR

The energy carried in the Sun's rays is absorbed by dark coloured panels and used to <u>heat</u> water.

matt black solar panels on roof

cold water in

hot water out

+ No pollution.

– Initially quite <u>expensive</u>.
– May not be so useful in regions where there is <u>limited sunshine</u>.

Examiner's Top Tip
Don't waste time memorising the diagrams. Do look at them and remember the advantages and disadvantages of each resource.

BIOMASS

The <u>chemical</u> <u>energy</u> <u>stored</u> <u>in</u> '<u>things</u> <u>that</u> <u>have</u> <u>grown</u>', e.g. wood, can be <u>released</u> <u>by</u> <u>burning</u> it. This energy source can be maintained by growing a succession of trees and then cropping them when they mature.

+ <u>Renewable</u> source of energy.
+ <u>Low-level</u> <u>technology</u>, therefore useful in developing countries.
+ Does not add to the greenhouse effect as the carbon dioxide plants and trees release when burned was taken from the atmosphere as they grew.

− <u>Large</u> areas of land needed to grow sufficient numbers of trees.

WIND POWER

The kinetic energy of the <u>wind</u> is used to drive turbines and generators.

+ It is a <u>renewable</u> source of energy and therefore will not be exhausted.
+ Has <u>low-level</u> <u>technology</u> and therefore can be used in developing countries.
+ No atmospheric pollution

− <u>Visual</u> and <u>noise</u> <u>pollution</u>.
− Limited to <u>windy</u> sites.
− No wind, no energy.

HYDROELECTRICITY

The kinetic energy of <u>flowing</u> <u>water</u> is used to drive turbines and generators.

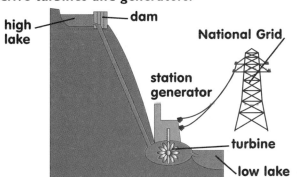

+ <u>Renewable</u> source.
+ Energy can be <u>stored</u> until required.
+ No atmospheric pollution

− <u>High</u> initial cost.
− <u>High</u> cost to environment, e.g. flooding, loss of habitat.

WAVE POWER

The <u>rocking</u> <u>motion</u> of the waves is used to generate electricity.

simple wave machine   the energy in the water waves make this machine rock

this motion is then used to generate electricity

+ <u>Renewable</u> source.
+ No atmospheric pollution.
+ Useful for isolated islands.

− <u>High</u> initial cost.
− Visual pollution.
− <u>Poor</u> <u>energy</u> <u>capture</u>. Large area of machines needed even for small energy return.

QUICK TEST

1. Name three ways in which water could be used as an energy resource.
2. Name two energy resources whose use which may pollute the environment visually.
3. Name two energy resources which could be easily used and maintained in developing countries.
4. Name two energy resources whose capture require a suitable site that might be rare.
5. Name one energy resource whose capture might cause an audible pollution.

1. Hydroelectricity, tidal, wave
2. Wind, waves
3. Wind, biomass
4. Geothermal, tidal
5. Wind

CONDUCTION

Heat is being <u>transferred</u> along this rod by <u>conduction</u>.

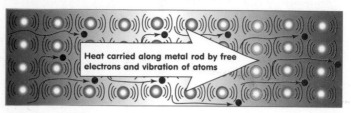

hot

Heat carried along metal rod by free electrons and vibration of atoms

cold

- Particles at the hot end <u>vibrate</u> and move around <u>more</u> <u>vigorously</u>.
- These <u>extra</u> <u>vibrations</u> are <u>passed</u> <u>on</u> <u>to</u> <u>neighbouring particles</u> causing them to move more vigorously.
- As a result the cold end of the rod gradually becomes warmer.
- All <u>metals</u> are <u>good conductors</u> of heat.
- Most <u>non-metals</u> are <u>poor conductors</u> of heat.

- <u>Gases</u> (air) are <u>excellent</u> <u>insulators</u>.
- They do no allow heat to pass through them easily.

- woven materials, e.g. wool and cotton, contain trapped air and are excellent insulators.

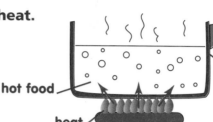

insulated handle

metal pan allows heat to pass through easily

hot food

heat

HEAT TRANSFER

Heat will flow when there is a temperature difference between two places. It will flow from the hotter to the cooler place. There are three methods by which it can do this. These are <u>conduction</u>, <u>convection</u> and <u>radiation</u>.

INSULATING THE HOME

- This diagram shows how heat may escape from a house that has not been insulated.

10% through windows, cured by installing double glazing.

25% through roof, cured by putting insulation into loft.

25% through walls, cured by having cavity wall insulation.

25% through gaps and cracks around doors and windows, cured by fitting draft excluders.

15% through floor, cured by fitting carpets and underlay.

CONVECTION

Takes place in liquids and gases.

Heat is carried to all parts of the tube by convection current.

3. Fluid cools, becomes dense and falls.

2. Fluid expands, becomes less dense and rises.

1. Liquid/gas is warmed.

RADIATION

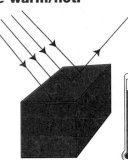

Heat travelling as rays.

- Objects with <u>dark</u>, <u>rough</u> <u>surfaces</u> <u>absorb</u> <u>most</u> <u>of</u> <u>the</u> <u>radiation</u> and become warm/hot.

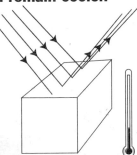

- Objects with light <u>coloured</u>, <u>shiny</u> <u>surfaces</u> <u>reflect</u> <u>most</u> <u>of</u> <u>the</u> <u>radiation</u> and will remain cooler.

- Houses in hot countries are often painted white so they <u>reflect</u> <u>the</u> <u>radiation</u> and <u>stay</u> <u>cool</u>.

QUICK TEST

1. Name three methods by which heat can travel.
2. Give one example and one use of a good conductor.
3. Give one example and one use of an insulator.
4. Why do metals always feel cold?
5. What is double glazing?
6. Suggest five methods by which you could reduce the heat escaping from your house.
7. How does heat travel from the Sun to the Earth?
8. What two things might happen when heat radiation strikes an object?
9. How is the heat from a radiator transferred to all parts of a room?

9. Convection current
8. Absorbed or reflected
7. Radiation
6. Fibreglass in loft, double glazing, draught excluders, cavity wall insulation, carpets and underlay.
5. Two panes of glass with air in between.
4. Conduct heat from body quickly.
3. Plastic, tablemat
2. Metal, saucepan.
1. Conduction, convection and radiation

CIRCUIT DIAGRAMS AND COMPONENTS

ELECTRIC CURRENT

- An electric current is <u>a</u> <u>flow</u> of <u>charge</u>.

- Charges can be made to flow using a <u>cell</u> or a <u>battery</u>.

- <u>Cells</u> <u>and</u> <u>batteries</u> act as <u>charge</u> <u>pumps</u>.

- They give charges <u>energy</u>.

- Several cells connected together can produce a <u>larger</u> <u>current</u>.

- Several cells connected together like this are called a <u>battery</u>.

- Care must be taken to connect the cells so that they are all pumping in <u>the</u> <u>same</u> <u>direction</u>.

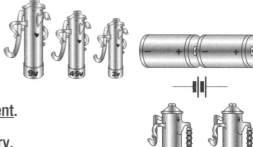

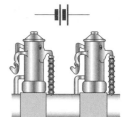

SIMPLE CIRCUITS

- **Charges can flow through <u>wires</u> in the same way that pumped water flows through <u>pipes</u>.**
- **The wires, cells, bulbs etc must be connected to form a <u>complete</u> <u>loop</u> (or circuit).**
- **If there are gaps the circuit will be <u>incomplete</u> and <u>no</u> current will flow.**

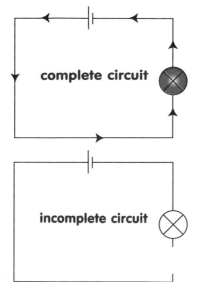

complete circuit

incomplete circuit

CIRCUIT DIAGRAMS

- Instead of trying to draw diagrams of the actual components in a circuit we use <u>circuit</u> <u>diagrams</u> containing easy-to-draw symbols for the components, as shown in the diagrams below.

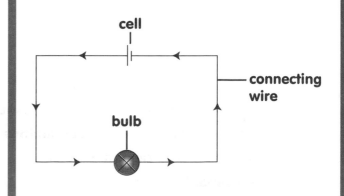

cell

connecting wire

bulb

CIRCUIT SYMBOLS YOU SHOULD KNOW

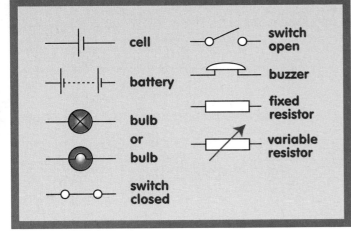

cell

battery

bulb or bulb

switch closed

switch open

buzzer

fixed resistor

variable resistor

SWITCHES

- Switches behave like <u>drawbridges</u>, making a circuit complete when they are closed and incomplete when they are open.

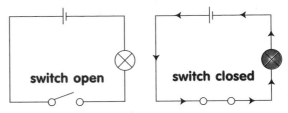

switch open   switch closed

- When the switch is <u>open</u> the circuit is <u>incomplete</u>, current will not flow and the bulb is turned <u>off</u>.
- When the switch is <u>closed</u> the circuit is <u>complete</u>, current will flow and the bulb is turned <u>on</u>.

CONDUCTORS AND INSULATORS

- <u>Metals</u> are <u>good</u> <u>conductors</u> of electricity.
- They allow charges to move through them easily.
- Non-metals are mainly <u>poor</u> <u>conductors</u> (or <u>insulators</u>).
- They do not allow charges to move through them easily.

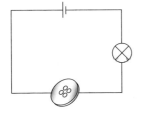 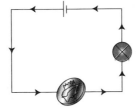

an object made from an insulating material will not complete the circuit

an object made from a conducting material completes the circuit

RESISTORS

- <u>Resistors</u> are used to <u>control the size of</u> <u>current</u> flowing through a circuit.
- With no resistor in this circuit the current is <u>large</u> and the bulb glows <u>brightly</u>.

- If a resistor is connected into the circuit a <u>smaller</u> <u>current</u> flows and the bulb is <u>dimmer</u>.

- If a <u>variable</u> <u>resistor</u> is connected into the circuit the size of the current flowing can be <u>altered</u>.

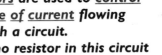

- The variable resistor is controlling the brightness of the bulb.

QUICK TEST

1. What is a battery?
2. What does a battery do in a circuit?
3. In order that a current will flow a circuit must be ....
4. Name one material that is a) a conductor and b) an insulator.
5. What does a resistor do in a circuit?
6. What is a variable resistor?

CIRCUITS – CURRENT AND VOLTAGE

MEASURING CURRENT

- We <u>measure</u> <u>current</u> with an <u>ammeter</u>.
- We measure current in <u>amperes</u> or <u>amps</u> (<u>A</u>).
- The size of a current is the <u>rate</u> at which <u>charge</u> is <u>flowing</u>.

- Ammeter 1 is measuring the current flowing through AB
- Ammeter 2 is measuring the current flowing through BC
- Ammeter 3 is measuring the current flowing through CD
- All three ammeters show that the same current is flowing in all parts of the circuit.
- This proves that <u>current is not used up as it flows around a circuit</u>.

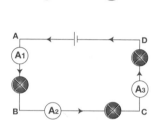

$A_1 = A_2 = A_3$

ENERGY AND CIRCUITS

- Charges are given energy as they pass through a cell or battery.
- The higher the <u>voltage</u> of a cell or battery the greater the amount of <u>energy</u> given to the <u>charges</u>.
- We can <u>measure</u> the energy given to the charges by the cell or battery using a <u>voltmeter</u>.
- The voltmeter is connected across the cell.
- As charges flow around a circuit they <u>give</u> <u>away</u> <u>the</u> <u>energy</u> they were given by the cell/battery.
- This <u>energy</u> <u>is</u> <u>transferred</u> <u>into</u> <u>other</u> <u>forms</u> by the components in the circuit.

V_{cell}
This voltmeter is measuring the energy given to charges by the cell.

V_1
This voltmeter is measuring the electrical energy changed into heat and light energy by the bulb.

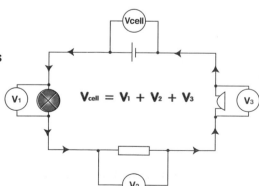

$V_{cell} = V_1 + V_2 + V_3$

V_3
This voltmeter is measuring the electrical energy changed into sound energy by the buzzer.

V_2
This voltmeter is measuring the electrical energy changed into heat energy by the resistor.

- A <u>bulb</u> <u>transfers</u> electrical energy into <u>heat</u> and <u>light</u> energy.
- A <u>resistor</u> <u>transfers</u> electrical energy into <u>heat</u> energy.
- A <u>buzzer</u> <u>transfers</u> electrical energy into <u>sound</u> energy, etc.

SERIES AND PARALLEL CIRCUITS

There are two types of circuit: <u>series</u> <u>circuits</u> and <u>parallel</u> <u>circuits</u>.

SERIES CIRCUITS

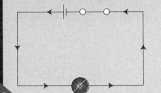

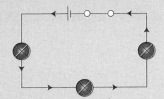

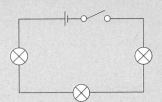

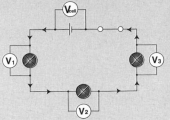

No branches only one path to follow.

Same current in all parts.

Switch open — no current anywhere in the circuit.

$V_{cell} = V_1 + V_2 + V_3$

- These have no branches or junctions
- They only have one path for the current to follow
- Can be turned on and off by a single switch anywhere in the circuit: 'one out all out'.
- They have the <u>same</u> current flowing in all parts of the circuit.
- The sum of the voltages across all the components is <u>equal</u> <u>to</u> the voltage across the cell or battery.

PARALLEL CIRCUITS

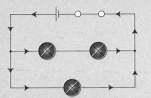

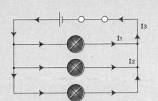

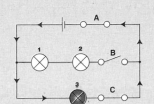

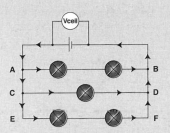

Currents may be different in different parts of the circuit circuits have branches and more than one path to follow.

Different currents but currents flowing into junction = currents flowing out i.e. $I_1 + I_2 = I_3$

Opening switch B turns off bulbs 1 and 2 but current can still flow through bulb 3. Bulb 3 can be turned on and off with switch C. Switch A can turn all three bulbs on and off.

$V_{cell} = V_{AB} = V_{CD} = V_{EF}$

- These have branches and junctions.
- There is more than one path for the current to follow. There is <u>choice</u>.
- Switches can be put into the circuit to turn on and off all or just part of the circuit.
- The size of currents flowing in different parts of the circuit may be different.
- However, the current flowing into a junction must be equal to the current flowing out of the junction.

Examiner's Top Tip
It is really important to understand the properties and differences of series and parallel circuits and be able to draw examples of each. Practise drawing circuits containing five or six bulbs with lots of switches and then explaining which switches control which bulbs.

QUICK TEST

1. What is an electric current?
2. How do we measure the size of an electric current?
3. In what units do we measure electric current?
4. What is not used up in an electrical circuit?
5. What is carried around a circuit by the charges?
6. What does a voltmeter measure when it is connected across a) a cell and b) a bulb in a circuit?

6. a) The energy given to the charges, b) The energy changed into heat and light by the bulb
5. Energy
4. Current
3. Amperes or amps
2. Ammeter
1. Flow of charge

MAGNETISM AND ELECTROMAGNETISM

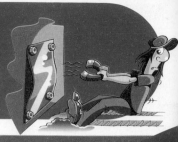

MAGNETS

- **Magnets** attract **magnetic materials**, e.g. iron, steel, nickel and cobalt
- **Magnets** do not attract **non-magnetic materials**, e.g. wood, plastic, copper, aluminium, etc.

magnet

magnets do not attract non-magnetic materials e.g. plastic, paper, wood, etc.

magnet

magnets attract magnetic materials e.g. iron, steel, nickel, cobalt

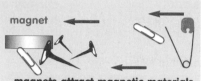
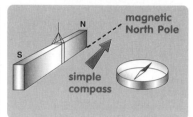

magnetic North Pole

N

S

simple compass

- The **strongest parts** of a magnet are its **poles**.
- Most magnets have **two poles**: a **North pole** and a **South pole**.
- A bar magnet suspended horizontally will align itself with the Earth's magnetic field so that its North pole points north and its South pole points south. The magnet behaves like **a compass**.

similar poles repel

| N | N |

opposite poles attract

| S | N |

ELECTROMAGNETS

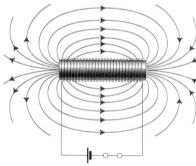

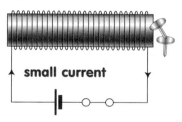

To make the magnetic **field stronger** we can:
- **increase the current**

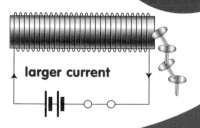

small current

larger current

- If a current is passed through a wire which is wrapped around a piece of iron a **strong magnetic field** is created.
- This combination of **coil and core** is called an **electromagnet**.
- The **magnetic field** around this electromagnet is the **same shape** as that of a **bar magnet**.

- increase the **number of turns** on the coil.

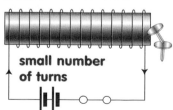

small number of turns

larger number of turns

- One of the main advantages of an electromagnet over a permanent magnet is that it can be turned on and off.

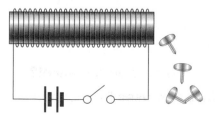

MAGNETIC FIELDS

- A <u>magnetic field</u> is a <u>volume of space</u> where magnetic effects, e.g. attraction and repulsion, can be <u>detected</u>.
- The shape of the magnetic field around a bar magnet can be seen using iron filings or plotting compasses.

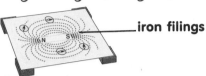
iron filings

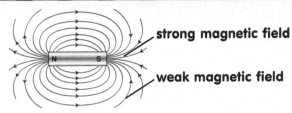
strong magnetic field

weak magnetic field

- The <u>shape</u>, strength and direction of magnetic fields is shown using <u>magnetic lines of force</u>.
- The lines are <u>close together</u> where the field is <u>strong</u>.
- The lines are <u>far apart</u> where the field is <u>weak</u>.
- The lines travel from <u>north to south</u>.

USES OF ELECTROMAGNETS

ELECTRIC BELL
- When the bell push is pressed the circuit is complete and the electromagnet is turned on.
- The <u>soft iron armature</u> is pulled towards the electromagnet and the <u>hammer</u> hits the <u>gong</u>.
- At the same time a gap is created at C and the electromagnet is turned off.
- The armature now springs back to its original position and the whole process starts again.
- As long as the bell push is pressed, the armature will vibrate back and forth striking the gong.

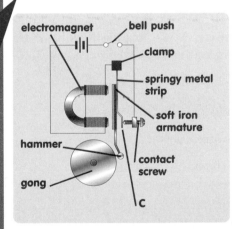
electromagnet
bell push
clamp
springy metal strip
soft iron armature
hammer
gong
contact screw
C

SCRAP-YARD ELECTROMAGNET

The soft iron core of this electromagnet is magnetised when the current is turned on but loses its magnetism when the current it is turned off.

- When current flows through the coil, a very strong electromagnet is created which is able to pick up cars.
- When the magnet is <u>turned off</u> the <u>magnetic field collapses</u> and the car is <u>released</u>.

Examiner's Top Tip
Don't try to remember how to draw circuits for the electric bell, the relay switch and the circuit breaker. Just try to understand how they work.

RELAY SWITCH

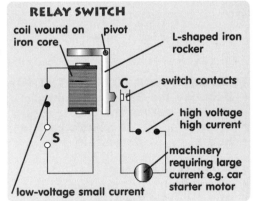
coil wound on iron core
pivot
L-shaped iron rocker
switch contacts
C
high voltage high current
S
machinery requiring large current e.g. car starter motor
low-voltage small current

- This is a safety device. It is often used to <u>turn on a circuit</u> through which a <u>large (potentially dangerous) current</u> flows using a circuit through which a <u>small current flows</u>.
- When the switch S is closed, a small current flows turning the electromagnet on.
- The <u>rocker</u> is pulled down and at the same time <u>the contacts at C</u> are pushed together.
- A large current now flows in the second circuit.
- When S is opened the <u>electromagnet is turned off</u>.
- The <u>rocker is released</u> and returns to its original position.
- The <u>contacts at C open</u> and <u>current ceases to flow</u> in the second circuit.

QUICK TEST

1. Name one magnetic material.
2. Name one non-magnetic material.
3. Similar poles ....
4. Opposite poles ....
5. What is an electromagnet?
6. Give two uses for electromagnets.

1. Iron
2. Plastic
3. Repel
4. Attract
5. A combination of coil and core.
6. Scrap yard, electric bell

THE EARTH IN SPACE

We live on a <u>planet</u> called the Earth. Although we cannot feel it, the <u>Earth</u> is <u>spinning</u>. The Earth completes one turn <u>every 24 hours</u> (one day).

This part of the Earth is receiving sunlight – it is daytime here

This part of the Earth is not receiving sunlight – it is night-time here

THE SEASONS

THE HIGHS AND LOWS OF THE SUN
- Because the Earth is turning, <u>the Sun</u> appears <u>to travel</u> across the sky <u>from the East to the West</u>.
- In the <u>summer</u> the Sun's path is <u>high in the sky</u>.
- In the <u>winter</u> its path is <u>much lower</u>.

THE SEASONAL TILT
- <u>The Earth orbits</u> the Sun <u>once every year</u>.
- Because the Earth is <u>tilted</u> we experience <u>the different seasons</u> – spring, summer, autumn and winter.
- When the northern part of the Earth is <u>tilted towards</u> the Sun it is <u>summer</u> in the northern hemisphere and <u>winter</u> in the southern hemisphere.
- When the northern part of the Earth is <u>tilted away</u> from the Sun it is <u>winter</u> in the northern hemisphere and <u>summer</u> in the southern hemisphere.

morning   summer (midday)   evening

winter (midday)

EAST   WEST

it is winter in the northern hemisphere

autumn

it is summer in the northern hemisphere

spring

spring

autumn

it is summer in the southern hemisphere

it is winter in the southern hemisphere

THE SOLAR SYSTEM

Our Solar System consists of a <u>star</u>, <u>a number of</u> <u>planets</u>, <u>moons</u>, <u>asteroids</u> and <u>comets</u>. We call <u>our star the Sun</u>. It contains over 99% of all the mass in our Solar System. The planets, their moons, the asteroids and the comets all orbit the Sun.

asteroid belt

Squashed circular orbits are called elipses.

All the planets revolve around the Sun in the same direction.

We see stars like the Sun because of the light they emit; we see planets because of the light they reflect.

- The Earth is one of <u>nine</u> planets. In order from the planet nearest the Sun they are: Mercury, Venus, Earth, Mars, Jupiter, Saturn, Uranus, Neptune and Pluto.
- We can remember the order using the sentence: <u>M</u>any <u>V</u>ery <u>E</u>nergetic <u>M</u>en <u>J</u>og <u>S</u>lowly <u>U</u>pto <u>N</u>ewport <u>P</u>agnell.
- We see stars like the Sun because of the light they <u>emit</u>. Stars are <u>luminous</u> objects.
- We see <u>planets</u> <u>and</u> <u>moons</u> because of the light they <u>reflect</u>. They are <u>non-luminous</u> objects.

GRAVITATIONAL FORCES

THE PLANETS

- The planets move in orbits because they are being 'pulled' by the gravity of the Sun.

the gravitational pull of the Sun keeps the planets in their orbits

- Objects which are closest to the Sun feel the strongest pull and follow the most curved paths.
- Objects that are further from the Sun feel a weaker pull and follow less curved orbits.

COMETS

elongated comet orbit

- Comets are large, rock-like pieces of ice that orbit the Sun.
- They have very elliptical orbits.
- They travel fastest when they are close to the Sun because the gravitational forces here are large.
- Close to the Sun some of a comet's ice vaporises, creating a long tail.

ASTEROIDS

- Asteroids are lumps of rock orbiting the Sun.
- They vary in size from several meters to about 1000 km.
- Most asteroids are found in a belt between Mars and Jupiter.

Key Terms!
Make sure you understand these terms before moving on:
* solar system * star * planet * moon * asteroid * comet
* gravitational forces * elliptical orbit * satellite

SATELLITES

- **Moons** are large natural satellites that orbit a planet.
- We have just one moon but some planets have several e.g. Mars has two, Jupiter has 16 and Saturn has 21.

Artificial satellites launched by man can be put into orbit around the Earth.
They have three main uses:

- To look away from the Earth into deep space, e.g. the Hubble telescope.
- To monitor conditions on the surface of the Earth, e.g. weather satellites. Satellites that monitor the Earth's surface are often put into low polar orbits.
- Geostationary satellites that stay above the same place on the Earth's surface the whole time, e.g. communications satellites.

INTERESTING (BUT NOT TO BE MEMORISED)

Quite often in an examination you will be given a table of facts about the Solar System and then asked questions about it:

Planet	Distance from the Sun (millions of km)	Orbit time in Earth years	Mass compared with the Earth	Surface temperature in °C
Mercury	60	0.2	0.05	350
Venus	110	0.6	0.8	/
Earth	150	1.0	1.0	22
Mars	230	1.9	0.1	−30
Jupiter	775	11.9	318	−150
Saturn	1450	29.5	95	/
Uranus	2900	84	15	−210
Neptune	4500	165	17	/
Pluto	5900	248	0.1	−230

Try these:
1. Name one planet that is closer to the Sun than the Earth.
2. Name two planets further away from the Sun than Jupiter.
3. Which is the largest planet in our Solar System?
4. Which planet experiences the strongest gravitational forces?
5. Estimate the surface temperatures of Venus and Saturn.

QUICK TEST

1. How long does it take for the Earth to complete one rotation about its axis?
2. How long does it take the Earth to make one complete orbit of the Sun?
3. What season is it in the southern hemisphere when the northern hemisphere is tilted towards the Sun?
4. Name one body in the sky which is a) luminous and b) non-luminous.
5. What forces keep all the planets in orbit around the Sun?
6. Where during their orbit of the Sun do comets travel fastest?
7. What is a natural satellite?
8. Give three uses for artificial satellites.

1. 1 day 2. 1 year 3. Winter 4. a) The Sun b) All planets and moons 5. Gravitational forces 6. When they are closest to the Sun 7. A moon 8. Looking into space, weather and communications

EXAM QUESTIONS – Use the questions to test your progress. Check your answers on page 125.

1. The diagram below shows two tug of war teams pulling on a rope.
    At the moment neither of the teams is moving.
    (i) What is the size of the force being applied to the rope by team B?

    500 N

    Team A   Team B

....

(ii) Explain your answer.

....

2. The diagram below shows a diagram of a periscope.
    Complete the diagram of the periscope by drawing in the path of a ray of light
    from the object to the eye of the observer.

3. The graph below shows the journey of a cyclist.
    (1) During which part of the journey
    is the cyclist not moving?

....

    (ii) During which part of the journey is the
    cyclist travelling fastest?

....

    (iii)How long did the whole journey take?

....

distance

E

C   D

A B

30   60   90   120

time in seconds

4. The diagram below shows a piece of wood labelled A being spun quickly
    whilst in contact with another piece of wood labelled B.
    There is a large amount of friction between the two pieces of wood.
    (i) Name two possible effects of this friction.

A

....

    (ii) Suggest one way in which this friction could be reduced.

....

B

    (iii) Suggest two ways in which the friction between a car tyre and a road may be reduced.

....

5. The diagram below shows a crowd of people watching a firework display.
    (i) Name one object in the diagram which is luminous

....

    (ii) Name one object in the diagram which is non-luminous

....

    (iii) Explain why during the display there is a delay between seeing and then hearing the fireworks explode

....

6.   If a bee flies close by we can hear its buzzing.
    (i) Which part of the bee creates these sounds?...
    (ii) Explain in your own words how these sounds travel to our ears...

7. (i) Name three fossil fuels..
    (ii) Name two environmental problems caused by burning fossil fuels..........................

....

    (iii) Name three alternative sources of energy...

....

8. (i) Explain why double glazing is far more efficient at keeping your house warm than single glazing with a thick piece of glass.

....

(ii) Explain why on a sunny day a black car becomes hotter than a white car parked at the side of it.

....

9. In which of the circuits drawn below will the bulb glow the brigthest?

10. The diagram below shows a magnet being used to try to pick up objects made from different materials

(i) Name 3 objects the magnet can not pick up.....................................

(ii) Why can the magnet not pick these objects up?..............................

(iii) What are the strongest parts of a magnet called?..............................

11. (i) Describe two ways in which the strength of an electromagnet can be increased.

....

(ii) Give two uses of an electromagnet.

....

12. Complete the table shown below

Energy in	Energy changer	Energy out
Electrical	Light bulb	Heat and ...A.....
Elastic	Catapult	.........B.....
.........C.........	Radio	Sound
.........D.........	Candle	...E..... and ...F......

13. A skier travels 200m in 5s.

(i) Calculate her speed...

(ii) If she continues to travel at the same speed how far will she travel in the next 10s?

....

0.3m

14. The diagram opposite shows a spanner being used to undo a nut.

(i) Calculate the moment created by the force.........................

(ii) Suggest two ways in which the size of the moment could be increased.

50N

....

15. The diagram opposite shows a fakir sitting on a bed of nails.

Explain why the fakir feels less pain if more nails are added to his bed............................

Calculate the pressure created when a force of 200N is applied over an area of $5m^2$.

....

How did you do?

1 – 4	correct	....start again
5 – 8	correct	....getting there
9 – 11	correct	....good work
12 – 15	correct	....excellent

123

ANSWERS

Biology

1. a) Nucleus b) Cytoplasm c) Cell membrane

2. The Chloroplasts.

3. A red blood cell, transports oxygen around the body.

4. 1b, 2d, 3c, 4a

5. Flower, root, root hair, leaf, stem

6. The circulatory system

7. Male sex cells are in the anther, female in the ovary

8. a) Water b) Chlorophyll c) Oxygen

9. Reptiles

10. Gets churned up and mixed with gastric juices containing protease enzymes and hydrochloric acid.

11. In the nucleus of cells

12. Absorption

13. Thin lining, lots of them (large surface area), and good blood supply

14. Oak tree leaves ➡ Snail ➡ Black bird

15. Emphysema, bronchitis and lung cancer

16. a) Oxygen b) Water c) Energy

17. Plasma, platelets, red blood cells, white blood cells.

18. An artery carries blood away from the heart at high pressure and has much thicker walls; a vein carries blood back to the heart at low pressure and has thinner walls.

19. 1. Produces antibodies. 2. Produces antitoxins 3. Engulf some bacteria and viruses.

20. The thick lining of the womb, the placenta and the amniotic fluid surrounding the baby.

21. Muscles that oppose each others movement e.g. the biceps and triceps

22. a) Trachea b) Bronchus c) Bronchioles d) Alveoli e) Diaphragm f) Intercostal muscles.

23. Where the immune system has a memory for a particular microbe and can produce antibodies much quicker to destroy the disease.

24. Nitrates, phosphates and potassium

25. The female part of a flowering plant, made up of a stigma, style and an ovary containing ovules.

26. Selective breeding

27. The air we breathe out is cleaner, warmer, contains more water vapour, and more carbon dioxide.

28. 46

29. The transfer of pollen from an anther to a stigma

30. Carbohyrates, protein, fat, vitamins, minerals, fibre and water.

Chemistry

1. a) B or C
   b) D
   c) A

2. a) solid to liquid
   b) gas to liquid

3. D

4.

Object tested	Attracted to magnet
plastic knife	x
steel pin	✓
iron nail	✓
wooden ruler	x
aluminium foil	x

5. a) solution
   b) 105.5 g

6. c)

7. a) green
   b) blue and yellow

8. a) iodine
   b) bromine
   c) fluorine/chlorine

9. a) magnesium + oxygen ➡ magnesium oxide
   b) The magnesium combines with oxygen.

10. a) iron oxide, carbon monoxide, carbon dioxide
    b) iron

11. calcium carbonate ➡ calcium oxide + carbon dioxide

12. a) magnesium, zinc, iron, copper
    b) magnesium + zinc sulphate
       ➡ zinc + magnesium sulphate

13. methane + oxygen ➡ water and carbon dioxide

14. a) magma cooled faster at T
    b) V is made from sandstone, U is made from limestone

Physics

1. (i) 500N. (ii) The forces must be balanced

2. Path of light

3. (i) CD. (ii) BC. (iii) 120s

4. (i) Wearing away of surfaces and heat. (ii) Use a lubricant eg oil or water. (iii) Worn tyre (lack of tread), smooth road surface or wet/greasy road surface

5. (i) Exploding firework. (ii) People in crowd. (iii) Light travels much faster than sound.

6. (i) Its vibrating wings. (ii) The vibrating wings created sound waves some of which enter our ears.

7. (i) Coal, oil and gas. (ii) Global warming (greenhouse effect) and acid rain. (iii) Geothermal, tidal, solar, biomass, hydroelectric, wind and wave.

8. (i) It is the air trapped between the two panes of glass which is the real barrier to heat escaping from the house, not the glass. (ii) The dark car absorbs most of the radiation from the Sun and so becomes hot. The white car will reflect most of the radiation and so will be cooler.

9. C

10. (i) The matchstick, the piece of paper, the piece of cloth. (ii) None of these objects are made from a magnetic material. (iii) The poles of the magnet.

11. (i) Increase the current flowing through the coil and increase the number of turns on the coil. (ii) Electric bell, relay switch, scrapyard.

12. A……..Light, B………..Kinetic energy, C…….. Electrical energy, D………..Chemical energy, E……. Heat. F……Light.

13. (i) 40m/s, (ii) 400m

14. (i) 15Nm. (ii) Increase the size of the force applied to the spanner, use a longer spanner.

15. (i) The more nails there are in his bed the larger the area his weight is spread over and therefore the less pressure (pain) there is on each nail. (ii) 40Pa

INDEX